# A Family's Guide for Success

Gage

# Are You Ready for 9th Grade

## . . . Again?

## A Family's Guide to Success

**A FAMILY'S GUIDE FOR SUCCESS**

Are You Ready for 9th Grade

. . . Again?

A Family's Guide to Success

By

Onedia N. Gage, M. Ed., MBA

# A FAMILY'S GUIDE FOR SUCCESS

ARE YOU READY FOR 9ᵀᴴ GRADE... AGAIN?

"EDUCATION IS OUR PASSPORT TO THE FUTURE, FOR TOMORROW BELONGS TO THE PEOPLE WHO PREPARE FOR IT TODAY."

MALCOLM X

Gage

# A FAMILY'S GUIDE FOR SUCCESS

Gage

ARE YOU READY FOR 9ᵀᴴ GRADE . . . AGAIN?

# Dedication

Hillary & Nehemiah
We have a chance to get this right!

Focus, Faith, Favor!

To the students whose lives I have touched!

We made every day count!

Ericka

Brandy

America

Haley

Rodney

Chase

Kimberly

Jessica

Myeshia

Sean

Jazmyn

Alicia

Shannon

This is not an exhaustive list!

Gage

# A Family's Guide for Success

ARE YOU READY FOR 9ᵀᴴ GRADE . . . AGAIN?

# Other Books by
# Onedia N. Gage, Ph. D.

Are You Ready for 9th Grade . . . Again? A Family's Guide to Success
As We Grow Together Daily Devotional for Expectant Couples
As We Grow Together Prayer Journal for Expectant Couples
As We Grow Together: Workbook for Expectant Couples Her Workbook
As We Grow Together: Workbook for Expectant Couples His Workbook
The Best 40 Days of Your Life: A Journey of Spiritual Renewal
The Blue Print: Poetry for the Soul
From Fat to Fit in 90 Days: A Fitness Journal
From Two to One: The Notebook for the Christian Couple
Hannah's Voice: Powerful Lessons in Prayer
Her Story: The Legacy of Her Fight The Devotional
Her Story: The Legacy of Her Fight The Legacy Journal
Her Story: The Legacy of Her Fight Prayers and Journal
ILY! A Mother Daughter Relationship Workbook
In Her Own Words: Notebook for the Christian Woman
In Purple Ink: Poetry for the Spirit
The Intensive Retreat for Couples for Her
The Intensive Retreat for Couples for Him
Living a Whole Life: Sermons which Promote, Prompt and Provoke Life
Love Letters to God from a Teenage Girl
The Measure of a Woman: The Details of Her Soul
The Notebook: For Me, About Me, By Me
The Notebook for the Christian Teen
On This Journey Daily Devotional for Young People
On This Journey Prayer Journal for Young People
On This Journey Prayer Journal for Young People, Volume 2
One Day More Than We Deserve Prayer Journal for the Growing Christian
Promises, Promises: A Christian Novel
Queen in the Making: Bible Study for Teen Girls
Six Months of Solitude: The Sanctity of Singleness Notebook
Tools for These Times: Timely Sermons for Uncertain Times
With An Anointed Voice: The Power of Prayer
Yielded and Submitted: A Woman's Journey for a Life Dedicated to God
Yielded and Submitted: A Woman's Journey for a Life Dedicated to God Intimate Study
Yielded and Submitted: A Woman's Journey for a Life Dedicated to God Prayers and Journal

Gage |

A FAMILY'S GUIDE FOR SUCCESS

## Library of Congress

Are You Ready for $9^{th}$ Grade . . . Again?

A Family's Guide to Success

All Rights Reserved © 2014, 2017

Onedia N. Gage, Ph. D.

No part of this of book may be reproduced or transmitted in
Any form or by any means, graphic, electronic, or mechanical,
Including photocopying, recording, taping, or by any
Information storage or retrieval system, without the
Permission in writing from the publisher.

Purple Ink, Inc. Press

For Information address:
Purple Ink, Inc.
P O Box 300113
Houston, TX 77230

www.purpleink.net ♦ onediagage@purpleink.net
www.onediagage.com ♦ onediagage@onediagage.com

ISBN:

978-1-939119-44-5

Printed in United States

ARE YOU READY FOR 9TH GRADE... AGAIN?

# Foreword

Imagine yourself sitting around the kitchen table with a cup of coffee, talking with your best friend about the best way for you to help your child(ren) experience academic success in school. Well, imagine no more. This is exactly what you will experience as you read, "*Are You Ready for 9$^{th}$ Grade Again? A Family Guide to Success*" by **Onedia N. Gage**. Gage has written this informative book in a no-nonsense, easy to read format (with just the right touch of humor), to ensure that the reader is "called to action," eager to implement the many practical ideas she shares. Although written primarily for parents of children entering the critical first year of high school, this book has much to offer all stakeholders committed to the educational success of our children who she describes as "our future EVERYTHING."

As an educator with more than 45 years teaching experience at both the elementary and university levels, I know that parents have an important role to play to ensure that their children are academically successful. Although great teachers do not use lack of parental support as an excuse for poor student achievement, we know our work would be much easier with it. This book is designed to enable parents to use their "parent power" to work hand-in-hand with their children's teachers to release the God-given potential inside all children.

The book, "*Are You Ready for 9$^{th}$ Grade Again? A Family Guide to Success,*" addresses such practical matters as graduation

## A FAMILY'S GUIDE FOR SUCCESS

requirements, the importance of state testing, the significance of the high school GPA, and the Texas state curriculum as it relates to what children must learn in high school. However, it also covers such topics as, *Motivating Your 9th Grader*, *The Value of Educational Self-Esteem*, and the often sensitive area of *Parent-Teacher Conference/Communication*. For example, specific guidelines are given detailing what parents should do during the conference, as well as questions parents should ask to communicate more effectively with their children's teachers. Additionally, for those who would like to "dig deeper" into some of these topics, an extensive list of articles, books and websites are provided by the author.

*"Are You Ready for 9th Grade Again? A Family Guide to Success"* is a practical "workbook" for parents to use as their children progress through the four years of high school AND beyond. Gage's experiences as a mathematics teacher, student advocate and parent coach make this book a valuable resource for ANYONE who values the education of OUR children . . . and yes, there is even something in this book for students.

Cherry Ross Gooden, Ed.D.
Retired Associate Professor of Education
College of Education/Texas Southern University
Educational Consultant/Motivational Speaker
Houston, Texas

## Are You Ready for 9th Grade... Again?

## Dear Student,

THIS IS YOUR EDUCATION! For that reason, you need to engage in your education. I know that your education can be hard but this is for you. If you become an adult as planned, you will need at least 85% of what you have learned. If nothing more than for the educational support to your own children.

Education offers you the opportunity to change your legacy. In this economy, there are millions of people that are labeled as being in poverty. If we are educated, then we have a greater chance of moving out of that category.

You are the student! This is your future. Educational standards are established by educated, elected, and paid individuals and whether we agree or not, we need to meet the standards.

As a student, your goal is to be educated. Your requirements for yourself should exceed what is out there for you. You should have a hunger and a work ethic toward your own future.

Please start to envision that school as your safe-place to learn and experience new information. In the world, you are not able to do this at will, so use school to get this education as provided. The world can reject you and label you as unknowledgeable. This will continue to keep you unsuccessful. Decide to be the student who strives for excellence. When you are in class, please do

## A Family's Guide for Success

not disrupt instruction. Do not shut down during class instruction. Finally, you want to insure that you ask questions and come to tutorials for any extra help you NEED.

In some cases, you cannot afford to have your teacher quit on you because that may be the person that consistently is on your side.

Education comes before emotion, even in the dictionary, so leave your feelings for the topic and the teacher at home. Poor emotions can block your learning.

Good Luck!

*Onedia N Gage*

Onedia N. Gage, Ph. D.

Leader, Educator, Advocate, Coach

## Are You Ready for 9th Grade... Again?

# Dear Parent,

Some of you are exhausted and about to pull your hair out. Others of you are moving right along and all is well. Often there are those who are asking themselves what is going on.

First and foremost, you are the PARENT, which by definition is the first advocate in your child's life. For some of us, this is new and foreign and some of us have not taken it well.

Your child considers education the same way that you do. If you are laid back, chances are that they will do the same. If you communicate that education is priority, then your child will also make education the priority it deserves to be. Likewise, they will understand how to understand your expectations. These expectations address submitting assignments on time, paying attention in class, asking the appropriate questions and attending tutorials as needed. This would also include arriving to class on time, being respectful of the teacher, and being aligned to the conduct at school. They may even go the extra mile at times based on their interests. I will admit and support that parenting is harder than it has ever been.

I look forward to working with you for your child's success and by extension you own. This is a great time to recreate yourself. A great time to use

# A Family's Guide for Success

what you learned to better your child. Even though your school experience may have been less than great, do everything you can, especially what was NOT done for you, for your child. This effort will mean a great deal in the long run.

Parents remember you are grooming an adult. You are creating a long-lasting work ethic and great habits which are hard to break later. We are training them for the work force and we need a solid citizen. Whoever your child grows up to be is a reflection of you – no matter the circumstances. We need to give our best effort at this output for the child.

Our children are the next EVERYTHING! I am here to work with you! Remember, whatever grade your child is in is what grade you will recall at that time. So now you are a 9$^{th}$ grader again!

Sincerely,

*Onedia N Gage*

Onedia N. Gage, Ph. D.

### ARE YOU READY FOR 9ᵀᴴ GRADE ... AGAIN?

## Dear Administrator/Counselor/Educator,

I admire your 187 day journey each year. As a teacher and school leader, I empathize with your job and your struggles.

For the next 180 days/75,600 minutes of this school year, I challenge you to continue to fight for their hearts and brain especially when it is difficult. This challenge will be difficult however; I do know that students surprise us all of the time. Likewise, they eventually GET IT! We have to re-center them on education! We have made some critical changes with great intentions; however that is not quite the case. We have lowered expectations, added a false sense of security with the "no-zero" rule and allowed them to dictate the educational culture because of some who do not accept challenge or authority. We are failing ourselves because without the educational standards which we grow up with, we are actually underserving our students.

These students are our future...EVERYTHING! Whatever we graduate and put in the workforce, we are totally responsible for. They are the future elected officials and the voters. We need to consider that as we move forward before reducing standards, and harboring ignorance. When school districts are voting whether or not an earned grade can actually be recorded in the grade book, we have missed the mark. As administrators, my charge to you is to remain focused on what real education produces. We cannot afford our

## A FAMILY'S GUIDE FOR SUCCESS

students—no matter what goes on around them outside of 7am-4pm, Monday-Friday—to be excused from excellence.

Lastly, I want to encourage you that we are in the race to win their minds and hearts and we are not losing. We are gaining ground overall. We need to continue to work hard at educating our students.

Keep your heart in it! Our students need your hearts!

Our parents need your wisdom and guidance. Somewhere between graduating and their kids going to high school, the parents have forgotten the requirements of graduation, attendance, participation, and academic excellence. Don't quit until we have earned their hearts.

Sincerely,

*Onedia N Gage*

Onedia N. Gage, Ph. D.

Are You Ready for 9th Grade... Again?

# Through Children's Eyes
## By Onedia N. Gage, Ph. D.

The purity that exists
Which dwells within
Through children's eyes
Tell the story of their life

The innocence that exists
Which expresses their honesty
From children's eyes
Shares their knowledge

The trust that exists
Which develops from their soul
From children's eyes
Communicates the level of trust which inhabits them

The love they need
Which grows within
Through children's eyes
Requests the love they need from you

The love they have
Which they give away freely
Through children's eyes
Shares the love they have for you

The innocence of their eyes
Solves problems
Calms fears
Steals hearts
Stills the soul
Changes minds
Settles disputes

## A Family's Guide for Success

The power they have
Through their eyes
Shapes lives

**Printed in <u>In Purple Ink: Poetry for the Soul</u> by**

**Onedia N. Gage, Ph. D.**

ARE YOU READY FOR 9ᵀᴴ GRADE . . . AGAIN?

# Why This Book

Based on all other materials in this vast world of literature designed for parents and education, this book is a call to action!

This book is a challenge! To the parent, then to the student, then the rest of the team, including the educator(s) and family.

This book is designed to turn the "ship" around. Your child is in need of assistance and you are the first to assist. We need you to re-engage with your child so that the very best can happen with your urging. This is a book which forces you to be present. You will need to be present and accountable for your student to succeed.

We are taking a direct approach about what a child needs to be successful. When we consider why this book, this is an authentic approach for education. We need to dive into our student's education but we will not discuss the statistics about education. This approach is one for the parent who just needs great information without the educational jargon and without the overwhelming attitude that your kid cannot possibly make it because of all of the circumstances which are against them.

This book is designed to hold you accountable, build confidence, establish a higher legacy, and benefit from hard work.

Gage |

## A Family's Guide for Success

It is easy to read with great, real examples in order to cement the information.

# Table of Contents

| | |
|---|---|
| Foreword | 13 |
| Letters | 15 |
| "Through Children's Eyes" | 21 |
| Why This Book? | 23 |
| Start with the End in Mind | 29 |
| Graduation Requirements | 37 |
| State Testing | 45 |
| State Curriculum | 53 |
| "It's Just High School" | 57 |
| Teacher vs Your Child | 67 |
| Success Has to Start Somewhere | 77 |
| "Where will I ever see this material again?" | 89 |
| The Value of Educational Self-Esteem | 101 |
| The Value of Education | 107 |

## A Family's Guide for Success

| | |
|---|---|
| Educational vs Emotional | 121 |
| Motivating Your 9th Grader | 133 |
| Parent-Teacher Conference/Communication | 147 |
| The Student | 167 |
| Achievement: A Matter of Legacy | 187 |
| Conflict Management | 199 |
| The Successful 9th Grader | 211 |
| $10^{th}$, $11^{th}$, and Senior Year: What Happens If We Need to Catch Up | 225 |
| It's Not That Long—4 More Years | 232 |
| Conclusion | 241 |
| Resources | 243 |
| Acknowledgments | 245 |
| About the Educator | 247 |

### ARE YOU READY FOR 9TH GRADE... AGAIN?

"ONLY THE EDUCATED ARE FREE."

EPICTETUS

Gage

**A FAMILY'S GUIDE FOR SUCCESS**

ARE YOU READY FOR 9TH GRADE... AGAIN?

# Start With the End in Mind

**What is the Goal?**

High school is the last stop before legal adulthood occurs. This is a critical 720 classroom days from day one to graduation day. The total 1461 days are critical to the overall outcome. The impact of these days is life-long. Not a day goes by when your high school journey is not a part of your daily life. As an adult, we have realized that there were days we wasted during high school because now we need that information and the experience that we missed. While we are cannot regain that time, we can exercise our knowledge and maturity by sharing with and ensuring through our children that they benefit from our experience and activities. In summary, we need to help our students understand that this time is substantially important and will not be repeated. They will not get this time back. The way that this time is designed will never be available passed this point.

The goal is to complete school with as much information as possible which is to be used at various times; including when they have children who need help with their homework.

The goal is to be equipped and adequately educated to be a contributing member of this society. The goal includes raising your self-esteem, being educated enough to carry-out your daily job functions, your home life, and being

## A FAMILY'S GUIDE FOR SUCCESS

able to help your child with his homework. The goal is to not be defensive because you do not know something that was taught. The goal is a knowledgeable workforce. This high school education seems insignificant for some, but for others, this is simply a spring board into the start of a great life, through career, future education and family.

The goal is to change a poor legacy. If we are honest as a parent, we know two things: first, we made some mistakes as a child that we wish that we could go back and fix, such as use our time more wisely as a student, and secondly we want our children to have better opportunities than we did. This is their opportunity to change their future, and they can maximize their education so that time will be well spent and well maintained.

The goal is a SUCCESSFUL STUDENT! Realize that I did not say smart, I said successful. The definition of a successful student is one who matriculates through high school who feels good about the experience and looks back on the school experience as a good one.

Lastly, the goal is to hold your head up rather than down when your child(ren) ask you were you a great student or what kind of grades did you earn, or my favorite, can you help me with my homework? These are key to your relationship and credibility with your student. While this may not mean anything to you today, this will be valuable later in life.

## ARE YOU READY FOR 9TH GRADE... AGAIN?

**How is That Achieved?**

Well, this may appear like a tall order for some of us; however, this is not impossible to be a successful student.

1. Study

2. Read

3. Homework

4. Ask for help in class and at other opportunities

5. Attend tutorials as needed

6. Be respectful

7. Pay attention in class

8. Complete all assignments

9. Try everything that is placed before you

10. Have a positive attitude

11. Do not give up and do not ever quit

12. Find an advocate for your student or yourself

13. Tell the truth about your education

## A FAMILY'S GUIDE FOR SUCCESS

14. Own your education

15. Do not make excuses

16. Do not blame others for your needs or what you lack, seek assistance

17. Harness your desire for a bad attitude

18. Remember you are in school! Not anyone else.

19. Be conscious of the cultural accountability. You have an opportunity that the generations before you did not. Right now you do not realize how important this is.

20. Do your best at all times!

    Action! TAKE ACTION! Your education is an investment, one that pays you regularly and intentionally. You never know what you will need or when you will need it. There is a statement that states I would rather have it and not need it, than need it and not have it!

    Education can be hard work, but it is well worth it. It is only 1480 more days. You need to be prepared for your future. Make the correct decision about your activity so that these days will not be ones of regret.

    As a student, we need to be reminded that you need to focus on what is in front of you. As a parent, we need to help them to focus while in school. As

## ARE YOU READY FOR 9TH GRADE... AGAIN?

a teacher, our hope is that you will not disturb them during the day by texting or otherwise and likewise discourage them from doing the same. Some of our best stories relate to "I was texting my momma," as I take the cellular device which was prohibited to be used in class, and then the parent has to appear and pay $15 to retrieve the phone. Success requires your effort daily. It is not immediate or effortless! Success requires your time and energy.

As we share with your children all of these great aspects and details, I want to share this story with you.

A student was a great athlete and was the star of the team. He showed great promise. However, he graduated without the minimum SAT score required to enter college at a division 1 school. So all of that "talent" went to waste because we did not take care of what was between his ears. Eventually, he did get a degree however, he never did play division 1 or professional football – all because he did not find education important enough to make it a priority. Further, his parents were not able to help him because they did not know how to help him.

Gage

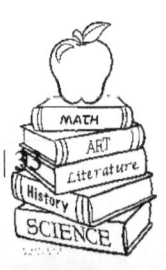

**A FAMILY'S GUIDE FOR SUCCESS**

**ARE YOU READY FOR 9TH GRADE ... AGAIN?**

"LIVE AS IF YOU WERE TO DIE TOMORROW. LEARN AS IF YOU WERE TO LIVE FOREVER."

MAHATMA GANDHI

**A FAMILY'S GUIDE FOR SUCCESS**

Are You Ready for 9th Grade ... Again?

# Graduation Requirements

The National Office of Education – the Department of Education establishes the Graduation Requirements. The President of the United States appoints the Secretary of Education. The Secretary is usually an educator with extensive educational experience.

This person is responsible for the content of www.ed.gov. Further, all of the material and requirements and directives which are given to the states also originate from this office. Graduation requirements vary by the level of educational accommodations for each student. The range of graduation requirements is from 22 to 26 credits. The variations include foreign languages, and the number of math and science classes. In an average high school, the school is on a seven classes per day schedule. For four years, that would be 28 credits — seven complete credits per year times four years. The outcome is based on your student's desire to achieve.

The requirements are flexible for two reasons: so that our students can be successful and so that they have some options on how to achieve that success.

The following states are among the top educational sources for several reasons. These are the sources for how to lead the state in educational

Gage

## A FAMILY'S GUIDE FOR SUCCESS

excellence. Use these to research what happens there so that you can understand how to reach what seems impossible.

1. Massachusetts        www.doe.mass.edu
2. New York             schools.nyc.gov
3. Texas                www.tea.state.tx.us
4. Florida              www.fldoe.org
5. California           www.cde.ca.gov
6. Iowa                 educateiowa.gov
7. Georgia              www.gadoe.org
8. Illinois             www.isbe.net
9. Delaware             www.doe.k12.de.us
10. North Carolina      www.ncpublicschools.org

The basic requirements include Math, English, Social Studies, and Science. The recommended graduation plan in Texas includes the "4x4," now known as 'House Bill 5,' which is four credits in each of these content areas, so sixteen of the twenty-six required credits for the recommended graduation plan

## ARE YOU READY FOR 9TH GRADE... AGAIN?

are core classes. The twenty-two credit plan excludes the foreign language requirement.

Consider that in a seven-class-period-day, in four years, there is the possibility of twenty-eight credits. This credit possibility also allows for the possibility of failing classes. Those credits are designated for English, Mathematics, Social Studies, Science, language other than English (LOTE), physical education, fine arts, speech, and some other requirements.

This is a comprehensive measure of the academic needs of the student for a functioning adult. These requirements and educational standards are what in part establishes us as the world's superpower.

America is currently ranked 25th in the world for education. We have to consider how those numbers are generated. 25th is not the ranking we are proud of based on many factors.

Massachusetts is the number one state in education in the United States. A major part of the criteria for this ranking is the results on the ACT and SAT tests. The educational acumen of each state is also measured by the results of state standardized tests. The states are required and monitored by the department of education for certain standards. There are times when Presidents initiate educational changes as well. We are currently under the Obama

## A FAMILY'S GUIDE FOR SUCCESS

administration reform of No Child Left Behind, which was a famous, failed Bush initiative.

Whatever the initiative is, it should be about children learning. As a parent, it is our responsibility to know what is required for our children to be considered educated. Standards have changed since you were a student. It will be wise to insure that we have made the necessary emotional, mental and physical adjustments necessary to make a successful impact for our children.

Graduation requirements include the state standardized tests. Many students have failed these tests which have their delayed graduation, so now they have determined that the process of education should have been taken much more seriously than they did during the daily opportunity of learning. The failed test prevents a student from graduating, which prevents them from proceeding with their lives. When the job and college applications ask if you have graduated and you say no, the denials start.

Graduation requirements vary slightly between states. The qualifications are designed to create a promising citizen who can survive the world. As a parent, I hope that you will join the team of educators in your child's life and assist them both with being successful.

Parents, you need to refresh yourself with the requirements and keep the focus on where your child is in regards to that standard. Parents, it is your

## ARE YOU READY FOR 9ᵀᴴ GRADE ... AGAIN?

job and your responsibility for your children's education. Please dismiss your past educational experience if it was not a good one. Now is your child's time for success. If your experience was great, then pass that greatness on to your child. Enhance that experience as well. Keep a chart of the school years so that you will be abreast of your child's progress. This is an investment in your future! If you do not have a handle on this situation, then you are gambling with some futures – for no good reason.

This time is a call to action! Your attention is required for this to go well!

Gage |

**A FAMILY'S GUIDE FOR SUCCESS**

# Are You Ready for 9th Grade... Again?

"I'M GOING TO INSIST THAT WE'VE GOT DECENT FUNDING, ENOUGH TEACHERS, AND COMPUTERS IN THE CLASSROOM, BUT UNLESS YOU TURN OFF THE TELEVISION SET AND GET OVER A CERTAIN ANTI-INTELLECTUALISM THAT I THINK PERVADES SOME LOW-INCOME COMMUNITIES, OUR CHILDREN ARE NOT GOING TO ACHIEVE."

— BARACK OBAMA

**A FAMILY'S GUIDE FOR SUCCESS**

ARE YOU READY FOR 9ᵀᴴ GRADE... AGAIN?

# State Testing

The most famous state tests are the Iowa Test of Basic Skills (ITBS) and the Stanford test which also ends with a number.

The purpose of state tests is to measure whether all of the states' students are academically accomplished at the same level. The students' performance indicates that which we deem important. The student's performance reflects the curriculum, instructional standards and the teacher's activities.

Texas has changed the name of its test four times since the inception of the test. What does the name change mean? Does the test's content change? Did the test's evaluation change? Does the test accurately report the knowledge of a testing student? Whether we believe in the test or not, it is the basis of our educational standard.

As an educator and as a parent, we need to understand that we owe to our children the best opportunity to be successful. Education is the difference between eating for today and eating for the rest of their days – with or without you. There were some disgruntled parents about some educators who were "teaching to the test." As an educator, teaching is a daily activity which your student is expected to learn, retain, and engage – DAILY! There is a test review

## A FAMILY'S GUIDE FOR SUCCESS

period and a preparation period, however do understand that this is a privilege and EXTRA! Educators teach DAILY! The test review and test preparation is an extra step, which is not required!

In 1979, in a school district which does not exist anymore, the administrative team simply sent a note home on Monday afternoon which stated that students would be testing for three days, to insure that we have a hot breakfast and a good night's sleep. The test was the next day. THAT WAS ALL!

What do you do as a parent, when your child has failed four consecutive semesters of math, on her way to her fifth? These tests are based on the subject matter standards. Expand your mentality and attitude about your child's education and the test! So when you consider "teaching to the test," be careful how you define, frame and criticize the method by which the teacher imparts information.

The tests are not going anywhere! They will keep changing, keep evolving, elevating in rigor and keep separating those who are educated from those who are not.

In Texas, it was rumored and believed that the number of prisons forecasted is determined by the number of third-grade test failures. While this seems outrageous, there needs to be the proper credibility to this erroneous

## ARE YOU READY FOR 9TH GRADE . . . AGAIN?

claim. The reading scores speak to the future of the success of the students. One such statistic is that not being on the proper reading level by the end of third grade translates into being four times less likely to graduate high school on time. If the student is from a low-income family, then not reading on the proper grade level by third grade is six times less likely to graduate high school on time (forbes.com). It needs to be considered that those students are judged by those results. Other states have an educational standard as well that they deem as a credible measuring tool for education.

There is a definite connection between literacy and incarceration. 60% of American's prison inmates are illiterate. 85% of all juvenile offenders have reading problems (forbes.com). While many states have denied this claim and there are no documents to substantiate the claim, these statistics suggest that proficient readers and literate individuals are less likely to occupy prisons. This is further supports that education is the key toward success and away from the horrible statistics which could capture our childen.

Whatever tests that are offered or required, there are basic areas that are standard: reading, writing, mathematics, science and social studies. We have expanded the definition of what is considered valuable; however the five basic questions we aim to answer on these tests are:

1. Do you understand the principles and definitions of English well enough to apply them to any written passage?

## A FAMILY'S GUIDE FOR SUCCESS

2. Do you understand the principles and theories of writing well enough to express yourself in a creative manner while staying within the writing page limits and compel the reader overwhelmingly?

3. Do you remember historical events in a premier manner while being able to parallel that history to current events? And finally,

4. Do you remember the rules, theories, postulates and processes of mathematics while comprehending what you are being asked to apply? And solve the problem efficiently? And correctly?

5. Do you remember the scientific processes taught to understand the human body functions?

Simply put: can you write? Can you read? Can you solve a problem? Do you understand what you read well enough to answer some questions correctly? Do you know why biology important? These are the same criteria in every school, each district, each city, every state – in this nation. That is what we want for each citizen, not an unreasonable expectation. Add. Subtract. Multiply. Divide. Read. Write. Understand. Apply. Remember. Retain.

When you see these words, why is there still the emotional upheaval? There should be none. Either our students can do it or not! The test is the same for districts who have a surplus or a deficit. It does not matter – the standards are the SAME.

## Are You Ready for 9th Grade... Again?

The test should not cause anxiety because it transcends color, gender, socio-economic, and race. The challenge is to focus on the education and the benefits thereof – NOTHING ELSE! It is unfortunate that we are focused on other aspects and have neglected pure education. Remind your child to attack their areas of weakness rather than build defenses or avoidance. Get help and be HONEST. If your child does not advocate for herself, advocate for her, not beg for her! The test will not be eliminated. Just perform!

Last word on testing: it is a snapshot of your child's knowledge. It is your responsibility to encourage your child to do his and her best. Each time. Your child is judged and instructed on this performance. If your child hates tests, then you should consider a few things: (1) does your child have test taking anxiety? (2) Does her/his knowledge fall short in the content area? And (3) is your engagement or lack thereof driving the achievement needed?

**A FAMILY'S GUIDE FOR SUCCESS**

### Are You Ready for 9th Grade... Again?

> "HOME IS A CHILD'S FIRST AND MOST IMPORTANT CLASSROOM."
>
> HILLARY RODHAM CLINTON
>
> <u>IT TAKES A VILLAGE: AND OTHER LESSONS CHILDREN TEACH US</u>

**A FAMILY'S GUIDE FOR SUCCESS**

ARE YOU READY FOR 9TH GRADE . . . AGAIN?

# State Curriculum

What does the state say the standards of education is? How much do you really have to know? Who do the states compete with to measure success when we consider education? How do we place a premium on education? How do we communicate that premium to the students we are measuring? Does the internet negatively affect the education we desire for our students? What stifles our children's education? It's not money! It's not location! It's not finances! So what is it?

A new trend is the 4x4. Four English. Four Math. Four Sciences. Four Social Studies. Whatever this means to each state, the common factor is the person who meet the grade for requirements and pass the test as a result of all that.

Foreign language requires two credits. Fine arts is two credits. Physical Education and Health are two credits. Other electives equate from two to four. That gives the students 16+2+2+2+2=24 graduating credits. All that matters is that you meet some graduation requirements to the satisfactory level mandated. The realization needs to be reached that we need to meet these because someone in your state has deemed it necessary to make these

## A FAMILY'S GUIDE FOR SUCCESS

requirements, and twelve others agreed that these were reasonable expectations of students.

Again, the curriculum consists of reading, writing, math, social studies, foreign language, physical education and some potential career electives. We are not asking for rocket science. Although, we may be hoping for more rocket scientists.

Again, these are more than reasonable requests for the education of our future adults. Check your specific state for exact requirements. National requirements can be checked at ed.gov.

**ARE YOU READY FOR 9TH GRADE . . . AGAIN?**

"EVERY CHILD NEEDS A CHAMPION."

HILLARY RODHAM CLINTON

# A Family's Guide for Success

Gage

ARE YOU READY FOR 9ᵀᴴ GRADE ... AGAIN?

# It's Just High School

It is just high school! That would be a valid statement if this same high school graduate were not able to be a military major or the lead at a construction site, which decides and approves and constructs how much re-bar goes into the freeway that supports me and my children each day.

There are approximately 720 days from ninth to twelfth grade: straight school, educational days. 1461 days total. 1461 is the total number of days from eighth grade to adulthood.

It is a very big deal. It is the biggest deal! At 18, our children are decision makers! Military. College. Professional sports. Workforce. Your home. Even at 18, we need to continue to encourage excellence.

We have 1461 days to help them make responsible adulthood decisions and choices. It's not just High School – it's four of the most important years of their lives. High school is the training camp for adulthood. It's not just high school: there are serious, life-changing decisions that follow.

High school usually creates career choices and opportunities. The choices are endless. Independence is established. Chances are you as a parent have not forgotten the overall experience. Further, the opportunities have tripled since you have graduated, so your experiences are not parallel. The child you

## A FAMILY'S GUIDE FOR SUCCESS

have is exposed to six times the experiences you were. Between social media, the internet and actual college/career fair visits, your teen is exposed to schools of which you have never heard. This exposure is to blame for your child's expanded knowledge base and contagious curiosity.

The influence teens have over each other is AMAZING! This influence is profound and far-reaching – further than the parent and other family influences.

As the parent/family, we have to insure that they have the proper influence over their friends and classmates for the focus on education. We have to keep education first and foremost in their lives. Education loses ground every day. Often the students feel that they do not need to retain information we present as educators because they can always use the internet to find the answers they seek. However, in their daily lives, they are not able to consult the internet for the answers their education requires. We are training THINKERS! We want our students/children to be thinkers and leaders.

Each of these students/children is our next everything – teachers, president, senators, congress persons, mayors, governors, CEO's, administrative assistants, and all other working personnel. When we consider our students and their education, this needs to be important! These are the persons who will vote and lead us in matters of economics and social services.

## Are You Ready for 9th Grade... Again?

Why is high school a big deal? High school is a big deal because this is the last four years you have with your child as a child. At this point, we have a small time to transition your baby into a responsible adult.

It is a critical time, and we need to focus them on their future life. We are to blame if they are unprepared or underprepared. This time needs to be used wisely so that we have a greater chance of success. These high school days are, usually, dreaded. This angst is driven by the newest hormone and attitude of the child, the additional expenses of this season, and the overall attitude of your educational experience. Your child adopts your attitude about education.

I meet many parents. When we meet, I can tell why the child has their attitude and behavior. If you excuse your child from total and comprehensive engagement in his education, then there is nothing that the rest of his educators can do to stimulate success and otherwise motivate them.

As the parent, she listens to your voice about education; however, your actions speak that an education is marginal in priority, however is an obligation dictated by the state government.

Your behavior dictates how these students will develop their behavior and attitude toward education. Consider checking their homework. Please check it carefully when you do so. Likewise, sit with her while she is doing the homework. Ask to see all assignments assigned for the class. Ask for the

# A Family's Guide for Success

syllabus. Check the teacher website for information on what the teacher suggests that your child needs to be successful. Ask how your child treats the teacher and how the teacher treats your child. Establish respect for the teachers with your child through your respect for them as well. Remember that the teachers are certified, educational professionals. The teacher should be treated as such. We need to consider how we train our children to respect adults. Many of the high-school students do not. From foul language to inappropriate questioning to complete disobedience, teachers hear it all.

Call your child's teacher and share any significant details as how to help your child to be successful. These details include inside information on serious learning conditions which have influenced the success or failure of your child. I have met many parents who did not realize how valuable this information is. As your share, you are speeding up the investment process the teacher works through to connect with your child. I make it my business to send a note or schedule a talk, either via phone or in person, about who my children are. I share their learning styles and their values – what motivates them. I share how to discipline them best and how to praise them. I share when I expect to be called/contacted based on their behavior and grades. I give the teacher an idea of what I think is important. In this dialogue, I share what I need to so that the teacher understands that I am serious about my child's education.

## Are You Ready for 9th Grade... Again?

Because of these proactive measures, I am guaranteed that I have done my share in supporting the teacher and my child in the educational process. This process does serve to eliminate the anxiety that exists with a new student.

This support is helpful for a successful education. This valuable insight encourages both the teacher and student. This conversation is a bridge for both of them. This handoff includes asking questions of the teacher and answering questions for the teacher.

It is just high school, so it is a training ground for the rest of their lives. High school is where they make the most friends. They learn the most information in the most concentrated timeframe. High school is the last guaranteed, formal education. High school is where she forms her work ethic, and his competition is being groomed. Likewise, you should afford your students the same opportunity.

High school is not an equal training ground. The curriculum varies between states, cities, school districts, schools and classrooms. As a classroom teacher, my expectations and standards were higher than others. This difference made me less popular. However, in the long run, my students realized they were more prepared than their colleagues. They visit me and thank me. It is my job as the educator to use what I have seen and experienced to educate and demand that they understand where they will see and use this concept again.

## A Family's Guide for Success

It is a complete disservice not to expect our students to excel and be successful, without excuse and disdain and complaint. I am often confused about the parent who comes to school and blames the teacher for everything, however the parent has not asked the entire school year for homework, assignments, report cards, or progress reports, yet all of these are indicators of your child's knowledge and progress. Then the parent demands that they are called to tell them what then parent should know through the computer grade book. When you show the students how to handle the classroom, then you teach them how to handle the boardroom. This time is critical for their successful future.

Work ethic is only developed through "exercise and repeat." Just like a human body muscle, it is only toned by exercise and repeat and increases intensity and consistency. You do not tone muscles or lose weight by working out once each month and certainly not by thinking about it or walking by the exercise equipment. Likewise, you cannot learn, retain, or apply these lessons by listening in class, rather than taking notes, reading those same notes, and completing all assignments. Our students cannot learn, retain, or apply by putting the assignments in their backpack and walking around with them – if out of sight then out of mind.

## ARE YOU READY FOR 9ᵀᴴ GRADE . . . AGAIN?

High school trains for the future. It should be treated as the important place it is. I watch at least a dozen students go to college then return because they were underprepared for college.

High school is your last real opportunity to exert your parental authority. Use it wisely and to your child's benefit!

Ponder this final thought:

How did Kobe Bryant, Kevin Garnett and LeBron James treat high school? As of this publishing, they each have over a decade in the NBA. They each manage millions of dollars. Those two details require hours of work ethic and preparation. Keep that in mind the next time someone says it is just high school.

**A FAMILY'S GUIDE FOR SUCCESS**

**ARE YOU READY FOR 9ᵀᴴ GRADE... AGAIN?**

"LET US THINK OF EDUCATION AS THE MEANS OF DEVELOPING OUR GREATEST ABILITIES, BECAUSE IN EACH OF US THERE IS A PRIVATE HOPE AND DREAM WHICH, FULFILLED, CAN BE TRANSLATED INTO BENEFIT FOR EVERYONE AND GREATER STRENGTH FOR OUR NATION."

JOHN F. KENNEDY

Gage

**A FAMILY'S GUIDE FOR SUCCESS**

ARE YOU READY FOR 9<sup>TH</sup> GRADE . . . AGAIN?

# Teacher vs. Your Child

As a parent, there is a balance that we must strike with regards to the teachers of our children. We are the litmus test for how they relate to others. We perpetuate that relationship. We need to insure that it is healthy, productive and whole. The "new-day's" teacher has quite the number of new demands on her job description. The "new-day's" child has additional distractions and elements which steer our students away from education as a priority.

The "new-day's" parent has both: a new role with ever-changing expectations with some new distractions to overcome to be successful. We are in this fight together. As a parent/educator, I have to work on both sides of the aisle.

As the parent, you are the orchestrator of this relationship. Please choose your tone and words wisely. Remember you are your child's advocate, however please do not use your parental power to put your child's teacher(s) on the defensive. The teacher is likely an advocate and an ally. Regardless of right or wrong, you need the teacher – all of them. Teachers are human, too. They live a life, too. They have trouble outside of their jobs from time to time, too. Understand that teaching is a job where compassion should exist and where

## A FAMILY'S GUIDE FOR SUCCESS

human lives are at stake. With that said, I want you to error always on the side of caution when communicating with the teacher.

In the "old-day," parents approached the teacher with an attitude of: 'I will correct my child. Thank you for sharing.' Now teachers are on the defensive and under attack. Consider this approach as a last resort.

Do use the BIG glasses as you build a relationship between your child and the teacher. People do things/favors for people they like. There may be times when you will need a favor in the form of extra credit and new assignments for your child. Help build a rapport that in the end protects you as the parent.

Consider the following and you decide how you would have handled this situation:

The student is failing Algebra I and Algebra I Intervention. The parent requests a meeting with the teachers. The first meeting was delayed because the teacher was called by another parent, so the parent was waiting at the office. After the mistake was realized, the teacher went to the office to meet the parent. The parent speaks to the teacher with disdain and disgust. The following words were uttered, "I am a manager at (major airline)." The teacher thinks, 'So what, you are a manager, but that management job is not helping your son in math.' The meeting is rescheduled and this time the counselor, the other math teacher

## Are You Ready for 9th Grade... Again?

and two assistant principals are requested as well. The student is failing because of missing assignments. As the meeting proceeds, the parent is upset and hostile with the original teacher and is openly showing it through body language and verbal insults.

The parent asked several times, "What are you going to do for my child?" The teacher replied, "We are going to continue to teach bell to bell, offer tutorials and communicate with you in regards to his progress." As the conference continues, and no real progress is being made, the parent states, "My child says he turned in his work, but you have not graded it." The assistant principal takes the child's backpack and retrieves all the contents and hands them to the teacher. The teacher sorts the documents by subject matter. When done, she pulls her stack toward her and compares the pile with the grade report to identify if the missing items are indeed present and they are. The teacher reports that the missing assignments, some of which he has more than one copy, are not only still in the child's possession but also INCOMPLETE. The parent should realize the child lied to her. The teacher stated, "I cannot grade what I do not have."

The parent asks, "What he can do to make this up?" The teacher replies, "Nothing. The late policy has passed, and grades are due in a few days. We have tutorials after school on Monday and Wednesday." The parent admits she cannot help him with his homework. The parent then says, "He cannot stay

# A FAMILY'S GUIDE FOR SUCCESS

after school because he takes driver's education." The teacher folds her notebook closed and crossed her arms. Her thoughts are, 'You have set your student up to fail, not me.' He has a lifestyle that is counterproductive to his successful education. You are here to demand someone do more for your child than you are personally willing and able to do. Is she serious?' Then the teacher recalls the parent stating that she was the manager of the airline. SO WHAT!!!

As the conference comes to a close, his other math teacher reveals that he is failing her class as well. The counselor reveals other areas of concern. Then the cell phone and other disciplinary issues are presented. The student lied to the parent. The parent acted on the word of the student although false. The student's actual work ethic was revealed. The parent was angry at the wrong person. The parent was embarrassed by her child's behavior. The parent was also hurting because she could not help her own child. The parent was overwhelmed by the entire experience.

Toward the end, the parent seemed remorseful but never actually apologized. Nothing changed as a result of that conference. Driver's education was completed. Assignments were still incomplete and in his backpack. He never attended tutorials. The parent never contacted the school again.

As the parent, would you have done anything differently? What should this parent have done at the end of that conference? Could the teacher have

## Are You Ready for 9th Grade ... Again?

done anything additional? Who holds the student accountable? He continued to fail.

As the parent, please advocate with a purpose. That backpack shows up at your home each day. How many days do you look through it and clean it out and read its contents and smell it? Often we as parents can prevent certain behaviors if we would invest at the proper level.

If your child is in need of academic assistance, then you are not the most important person in the room – your child, and the teacher are. Put aside who you are and what you have accomplished--none of that matters now. If any of your accomplishments and your status mattered, then your child would not need any assistance. This also means do not make the teacher seem inferior. The teacher is degreed and certified to stand before your child and is paid from public funds.

Invest in your child at home. Share your expectations with your child. Listen to what the teacher has to say regarding your child. Remember that the teacher actually spends more time with your child than you do. The teacher sees your child in the cafeteria, in the hallways, with their friends that they do not bring home and hear them say things that you will NEVER witness. The teachers know who they are dating, who they would like to date, know who they are dating, and that they are not supposed to be dating. Not to mention, the teacher knows who they were caught kissing under the bleachers.

Gage

# A FAMILY'S GUIDE FOR SUCCESS

Use this relationship wisely. This is the person who manages your child's mood swings and personality conflicts because the teacher cannot send her to her room or take her cell phone.

Finally, remember that you have a chance to change your experience by changing your child's experience. Offer them a different parent than you had – a better one. Face it, when your child comes home and says we played with the iPads today during math, you have to admit we are in a different environment. Stay focused.

Further, if your child is taking driver's education but is in the ninth (9th) grade, what are we saying?

Invest in private tutoring so that you can see and understand where your child is struggling.

Lastly, do not attack the teacher until you are willing to understand the complete situation. Use the teacher to get to know your child. The teacher has valuable information.

**ARE YOU READY FOR 9ᵀᴴ GRADE... AGAIN?**

"SUCCESS IS NOT FINAL, FAILURE IS NOT FATAL:

IT IS THE COURAGE TO CONTINUE THAT COUNTS."

WINSTON CHURCHILL

Gage

# A FAMILY'S GUIDE FOR SUCCESS

ARE YOU READY FOR 9TH GRADE... AGAIN?

# Success Has to Start Somewhere

**REINVENT Yourself**

9th grade is the start of high school, which means the start of the GPA. While this is not new information, most students do not think of it until the student is a junior. All of a sudden high school starts to be important. That fact is that we are late to the party!

9th grade is the grade to start our educational success! No matter what happen previously, 9th grade is the start. For the student who did not have the study acumen or overall ability, this is where we reinvent our student! This is a time to forget the past, unless it was great!

No matter what kind of student your child is, we will upgrade his status! The proposals included here within this book will share how to improve that performance. The start is important. The change is too!

An aggressive start is critical. Likewise, we had to change our minds and maybe even our personal opinions about the possibilities of your student. Later in this book, we share a great plan for success. While you may not do it all, you need to give effort of at least 80%. Your child's success depends on it.

Gage

# A Family's Guide for Success

By the way, Parents, GPA is still calculated the same. The GPA still starts on day one of 9th grade. We share this because some parents have displayed some amnesia. The author realized that the parents do not remember how this happens, much to the surprise of the author.

The GPA standard has risen however. There are some school districts with the GPA standard set at 7.0. The national standard is 4.0. This is used to rank the student's performance. That GPA is used to rank the students in your child's class. This GPA is used by colleges to determine who will be successful. The GPA will be the first factor but not the only factor.

## Work Ethic

Work ethic is defined as the effort and intensity and consistency of your work. Your child has to be taught how to study and how to manage the process of success. Work ethic is critical for the rest of our success. The study habits are the most under developed skills our students have. Poor study habits are evident when the teacher asks did they study. They return the question with a blank stare.

"How do I help them learn to study?" You ask! The answer is hard at best; however, we will trudge through the process. It is quite meaningful to know that this knowledge does not leap from the page or the voice to the mind of your student. Many students do not know how they learn and so they do not

## Are You Ready for 9th Grade... Again?

know to do that repetitively so that they can learn and retain what they have learned and know.

First of all, they need to see someone study, and they need to be taught to study. The mystery of studying needs to be revealed. So unless you are in school, you are not studying at home. We need to establish a place to read, work and do the problems. We need to sit with them while they do their homework, while they are trying to read, and they are trying to retain this information. So that means that you will not be texting or talking on the phone, however you will be sitting there attentively supporting the student. This is going to be very different for each of you. Your student needs your presence. This is unique because you did not have this type of support, and the worst part is that some of this information is foreign to you now. So the anxiety you may be feeling is real. The solution is to review your areas of need to reduce your anxiety. Refreshing your memory on the students' material is going to require some extra time on your behalf. It is important because you want to be able to help the student. When you cannot help, you need to have a tutor(s) on standby for this scenario.

Your presence is MOST important. Your presence speaks volumes about your commitment to this successful mission. Further, when you are sitting there, you are listening to offer encouragement to finish. You may need to answer a question or two, you may need to read a passage, offer your interpretation, and ultimately help the student remain focused. You may offer your student the opportunity for her to teach you what she learned that day. You have no idea how far this will go in your teen's heart and mind. The design is to create courage, enhance self-esteem, build confidence, and reinforce work ethic.

Work ethic is groomed and tailored. Study habits and effective studying are different for each person. The same amount of variations as with the type of learner your student is.

Study styles are outliner, narrative, or hints. Some people can memorize everything they hear and see. Others need to write everything down. Some need to take notes but need coaching on how to do so.

So we need to address this realistically. There may be a class on how to study and take notes. Likewise, we need to review how to outline a chapter in a textbook. These are not skills taught in high school anymore. The training our children need is not readily available as it once was.

Work ethic involves accountability. You have to be present to hold him accountable. Your presence is that accountability for both of you. Your presence should make success possible. Your presence also defines work ethic.

This needs to happen daily.

### Rewarding Work Ethic

# ARE YOU READY FOR 9ᵀᴴ GRADE ... AGAIN?

What motivates your student?

- Money

- Phone

- Gadgets

Your students are available for instant gratification and multiple levels of celebration. You need to establish a reward program, which covers long and short term rewards for achievement. Place these rewards on a poster on the side of the plan.

Short term is a phone upgrade at the end of the semester/quarter. You get the point of the reward program. You are similar. You like rewards, too.

At any rate, keep in mind that this is a change – HUGE. You are redefining education in your home and family. This new definition is going to inspire others to do the same. You just changed the standard in your life, and the life and future of your child. It is likely that you are changing the lives of your child's friends as well.

Only suggest/promise what your can deliver so consider carefully what you can do. Then work hard so you can provide what you have promised/agreed to.

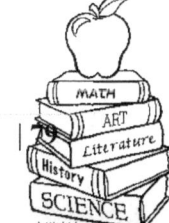

# A FAMILY'S GUIDE FOR SUCCESS

Make a list of what your student defined as a reward.

## Parents Share Your Story

## What is Your High School Story?

What kind of student were you? How would you change your experience? What would your teachers say about you? If your child could get a copy of your report cards, what would she say? Were you ever in trouble in school? Were your parents involved in your school experience? Were you in sports? In which sports, and/or other extracurricular activities were you active? What did you like about school? What did you dislike about school? What part, if any, do you regret from any of your years?

Are you proud of your academic performance? Will you share your genuine story with your student? This transparency is designed to inspire your student to success and achievement. When you share your story, ask your student to do HER BEST! Because of what your academic transcripts say, make it okay for your child to exceed your accomplishments and to do better than you did! Demand an outrageous excellence that only you can demand.

Your student will respect your candor and once equipped, will enjoy being "smarter" than their parents. It is very humbling for your child to ask your teachers what kind of student you were. Of course, the teacher is going to be gracious but how would it feel when what the compliment is genuine. Your

# Are You Ready for 9th Grade... Again?

child will be very proud to have a smart parent. Your child will be very proud to be a great student.

Share your experience with your child. Be truthful and transparent. Share what you learned, what you wished you known then so you could benefit now, and answer those questions. Do what was never done for you.

**Empower Your Child to Succeed**

Earlier, we advised that you make it okay for your child to be successful. Within the Hispanic culture, the children consider it disrespectful to be smarter than the eldest matriarch or patriarch in the family, particularly if he or she lives with the student.

Several students confirmed this which caused concern that led to research about the validity of the claim. While the parents were surprised about the children's perspective, they could not deny how they developed this thought or belief. The parents do understand how this happened.

Consider how cultural bias factors into education, more so than we realize. Culture is critical in family values; this is for education.

The students who shared their view also acknowledged that the parents made education very important. However, they were not successful. One parent asked if that was true. He confirmed the cultural perception and the strong

# A Family's Guide for Success

desire for their education were true; however some of the students were three years older than the average eighth grader. We had to put into action several plans to use our time wisely so that the students would consider success as an option. They were close to giving up.

Finally, the parent was asked in front of the girls, and the father announced to the girls that it was okay for them to be smart and successful. Her dad had to make it okay. Nobody could make it okay except him. Once he made it okay, the student performed differently – better, lifted her head, and achieved more. She just needed his consent.

Figure out how to empower your child. Encouragement includes notes, texts, celebrations, and rewards.

Teach your child something every day. Let your child teach you something every day. It is very powerful to exchange knowledge between the two of you. If you have more than one, teach them each something different. Let them teach each other what you taught them.

**ARE YOU READY FOR 9TH GRADE . . . AGAIN?**

"CHILDREN MUST BE TAUGHT HOW TO THINK, NOT WHAT TO THINK."

MARGARET MEAD

**A FAMILY'S GUIDE FOR SUCCESS**

ARE YOU READY FOR 9ᵀᴴ GRADE... AGAIN?

# "When Will I Ever See This Material Again?"

## Asks Your 9ᵗʰ Grader

"When will I ever see this material again?" is a popular question your student asks while in class before doing the work. This question is, usually, posed when the student is frustrated and is seeking some motivation for learning the material. If a student does not see the value, she rarely engages. The student wants to attach value to her education, and they are motivated by the right thing. However, they need to realize some of that attachment may come much later.

"Because is not the answer!" "Because the teacher is not teaching it," is not either. Neither is "because there is a test on it Friday."

The best answer is, 'Yes, you will see this information again;' when maybe as soon as tomorrow. The long-term answer is when you are a parent. The parents who paid attention in school are successful at passing that along. The self-esteem of that parent is better than average. This parent can exert her total authority over the educational acumen of her children because she is not afraid of what they will ask.

# A Family's Guide for Success

Parent teacher conferences are far more comfortable when the parent(s) does not say, "I cannot help my child with his homework! And I hated math! I do not remember that we learned algebra in elementary and middle school."

Those parents are sharing their need for knowledge and support. The student regards them differently, and their respect may lower. This is a huge risk for their relationship.

## Regrets for Not Paying Attention

Do you regret not paying more attention to the education you were learning? The author does. Biology was the worst subject! Meiosis and Mitosis are still taught in schools around this country. The internet is going to help the author to help her kids! That is the easy part. However, what about what she does not know.

After surveying several hundred people, 95% of them wish they could change their high school experience. This speaks to how we can impact your student's experience in such a manner that you could change her and future generations. For some students, they are the start of the first club: the first to graduate from high school, first to graduate college, and the first one to realize that education is important during the experience.

You have a chance to make a difference in your child's education. Tell them your story including your regrets and when you realized that you needed to be doing more. Let them know that you are here to insure that they have a better chance, and you will help to make it happen. You are pleading for the hearts and minds of your children so that the regret does not repeat itself.

## The Self-Esteem of a Parent Surrounding Education

When a parent cannot help his own child with the classwork and homework or answer any questions, the parent does not feel like a parent. The parent does not feel great about themselves. Likewise, the parent experiences regret for many reasons about the time that they spent in class. The impact of that regret is that it should inspire change and hope and achievement.

Please do not dwell there, however! If you cannot help them that means that we need to get some help: the teacher, school tutorials, and professional tutors. Yes, it will cost. A tutor may be out of your budget; however this is an investment in your child, your child's education, your child's self-esteem, and your child's future.

Parents do not give up hope! Start with the future in mind. Use your influence to drive your student to success. Abandon the downfalls that previously existed and the difficulty the future could hold and urge the student toward excellence.

You are responsible for your child's education, as were your parents. Maybe they did not do what they should, or they did what they knew to do –

Gage |

# A FAMILY'S GUIDE FOR SUCCESS

which may not be much. As a result, we missed some essential elements. We have an opportunity to fix our own lives at the time of our child's lives.

**Do not let pride stand in the way of educating your own!**

## The Parent Who Cannot Help Her Child

A parent came to visit on behalf of her son. The son was failing two math classes. Her claim was that her son was unfairly treated, intellectually neglected and academically ignored. She demanded to visit with his teachers, the assistant principal, and the counselor on behalf of her son. The parent had caused quite a ruckus, and she demanded her son be "helped." She further claimed that her son should not be failing. Her direct question to the teacher was 'what are you going to do to help my son?' The teacher paused for a moment before responding, "What is your son doing to help himself?"

As the meeting progressed, the assistant principal asked for the student's backpack. Upon opening the backpack, the extraction of the contents and the inspection, the parent discovered that she had campaigned for a child who had lied. The backpack contained the reason for his F. He had lied to his mother. He had not actually turned in the homework or classwork as he had reported to his mother, which had triggered her to call forth this "help." Further, he had more than one copy of the assignments – all housed in this backpack.

## ARE YOU READY FOR 9ᵀᴴ GRADE . . . AGAIN?

The parent was surprised. She realized that her son had lied and further embarrassed her. She mentioned that her son needed some support in math. The teachers mentioned that her son did not pay attention in class, and he requires frequent redirection from talking and texting on his phone. When is your child going to engage in his education?! The parent had no answers. She further asked what could be done to help him. The response was we offer tutorials on Mondays and Wednesdays from 2:45-3:45. Her response silenced the room. The parent said, "The student could not come to tutorials because he had to go to driver's education.' At that point, the teacher offered private tutoring for $45/hour.

The parent then admitted that she could not help her child with math. That should have been the most profound statement that she made during the meeting. However, there is no compassion for the failing math student who takes driver's education rather than coming to tutorials and paying attention in class. The parent just demonstrated that education was secondary. The child already knew that though. The effort of the family was exposed along with their priorities. The educator confirms that their efforts will match the student and parent, so the educator does nothing additional. The parent was not willing to do anything for her own child but expected others to do something "special." Not the correct behavior or example.

# A Family's Guide for Success

## The 7th Grade Student

The morning was fairly routine in the 7th-grade math classroom until the educator decided that those students who had not completed their homework would have to call their parents and report that their homework was not done.

One parent wanted a parent/teacher/student conference. As the teacher prepared for the conference, she gathered his work and test data. The conference was planned toward academic excellence and achievement. The parent and student had other plans.

This session became centered on the student's feelings. The parent introduced her concerns about how her son felt about the teacher. When she was asked for concrete examples, she was unable to share the situations. Further, the teacher then explained his performance in class, specifically how many assignments he handed in and did not attempt the work. The parent never addressed his lack of effort and participation; instead she returned to his feelings. It started to sound like his emotions were interfering with his education. This is a dangerous place because emotions should not factor into whether you are going to learn or not. The unfortunate part is that the parent did not have the philosophy to redirect the student. Since there was nothing specific that was shared, there was nothing the teacher could do. The teacher reminded the parent and student that the math is objective, so personal bias is not an existing factor. Further, the teacher reminded them that handing in completely blank assignments is not the best method for engaging in your education, and there is no bias in the grades earned.

The student then shared that he did not "hate" the teacher. The teacher found extreme humor in his statement because the student and maybe the parent were not focused on the education of the child. The student needed to realize that the person needed to address the personal nature of his education. The only person this affected was him. He was later transferred to another teacher. He failed 7th-grade math and attended summer school.

The parent is held accountable. As parents, our job is to protect our students, but sometimes that means protecting them from themselves. Her approach is not a wise one, where she has let him focus on his feelings about someone, and to interrupt his education, but the other students in the same classroom with the same teacher are overwhelmingly successful. The math is objective – you do the work, or you do not. Your grade is reflective and directly related to your efforts. It is not personal.

## The 12 Year Old Parent

Unfortunately, there was a 12-year-old parent in one class. The teachers had trouble with him sleeping in class and not completing the work. Those two elements are a recipe for failure.

## A FAMILY'S GUIDE FOR SUCCESS

The teacher approached the student and asked what was wrong, why was he sleeping in her class. He confessed that he had a baby, and she had been up eating, etc. As a result, he had not had any sleep for a few nights. The teacher shared with him that she needed him to focus, not for himself but her, the baby.

As a parent, the teacher appealed to his parental needs, while he was young, and the baby was new, he was still her dad. The teacher shared how she was able to maintain her children's respect and pride because she can help with their homework and answer the questions they have.

The teacher asked him how he would feel if he could not help her with her homework. He said not well and would be devastated. He then started asking questions about the topic and then about general parenting. The teacher understood the needs and addressed them as she helped him.

The student improved in his other classes as well. The teacher shared with the other teachers so they will know how to motivate him when he was discouraged.

The teacher team also considered ways to help the young man successfully parent and learn. The student thanked the teachers for not writing him off or quitting on him and for encouraging him.

## ARE YOU READY FOR 9ᵀᴴ GRADE... AGAIN?

Children are having children, and they really need the education presented. They are up against incredible odds.

**A FAMILY'S GUIDE FOR SUCCESS**

**ARE YOU READY FOR 9TH GRADE... AGAIN?**

"EDUCATING THE MIND WITHOUT EDUCATING THE HEART IS NO EDUCATION AT ALL."

ARISTOTLE

Gage

# A Family's Guide for Success

ARE YOU READY FOR 9ᵀᴴ GRADE . . . AGAIN?

# The Value of Educational Self-Esteem

Society is based on education. Education is labeled as the path to success. There are very few people who claim success without an education. Keep in mind that an education does not guarantee success defined by financial means and societal notoriety. Education is required for success for a healthy self-esteem. The education you have has dictated how you feel about yourself because your personal feelings are driven by others' feelings about you. While that should not matter – what others think – what other's think does influence how you feel about yourself. While that may be misplaced and inappropriate, it is true.

We have been driven and conditioned to pursue education so that we will be accepted and valued. While this drive is great for business, this is poor from a personal perspective. Your value as a person, parent and your child's advocate are not based on your education. But if you do not feel good about yourself because of your education, when make sure your child does not repeat this cycle. Your priority for your child's education is paramount. Likewise, if your child being smarter than you are a problem, then you have some choices.

One is to return to school and pursue your education to the level that you originally desired. Age is not an excuse; neither is time. Online and distance learning have become extremely accessible and popular for adults who

## A Family's Guide for Success

wish to increase their education. If you feel that you need education to feel better about yourself and more effectively parent your child, then return to school and achieve your goals.

What we cannot do as parents is keep our children from pursuing what we should have pursued with ALL of our beings. We have to give them consent to pursue what they desire and deserve.

The second option is to offer your child consent to exceed your educational level. You have to verbally articulate, "Child, please go to school and do WELL. Please, pursue all the education available to us. I want you to have more education than I have." They need to know that you will support and love them when they achieve this education. They need to know that you will not be hurt or offended if they have more education than you.

Please consider that you hold the key for their educational success. Please consider what you could encourage in the life of your child.

Please take a chance on yourself and your child for the life and legacy you can have. You have a chance to change the self-esteem of both of you.

Keep in mind that education can impact your financial and career opportunities. There are jobs that require a college degree. Most educators have a Master's degree, which means they have 36-52 additional hours of education.

## ARE YOU READY FOR 9ᵀᴴ GRADE... AGAIN?

You have found yourself lacking the education that you need for a position that you desire. When denial occurs often enough, our self-worth will be affected. Self-worth is what we want to impact for both you and your child. The pursuit and achievement of the desired and needed education will stop that cycle. That is the whole purpose of this thought process.

When your self-worth is in jeopardy, then so is your child's. It is hard to affirm your child when you do not feel affirmed or great personally. We are trying to uplift an entire family, an entire generation.

The cycle starts with your 9th grader! Inspiring your 9th grader and influencing your 9th grader toward excellence is our job. We are writing this book to change the future and forecasted behavior based on the student's previous academic performance. The changes we make should change the course of your lives. Education is a chance to create a new life for all of you. Change the mentality of you and your family regarding education. Education changes the outlook of the entire family. The outlook will seek to upgrade the entire family, and by extension, the community.

**A FAMILY'S GUIDE FOR SUCCESS**

**ARE YOU READY FOR 9TH GRADE... AGAIN?**

"EDUCATION IS THE MOST POWERFUL WEAPON WHICH YOU CAN USE TO CHANGE THE WORLD."

NELSON MANDELA

**A FAMILY'S GUIDE FOR SUCCESS**

Are You Ready for 9ᵀᴴ Grade . . . Again?

# The Value of Education

Education is ultimately important. The education you earn and retain is useful for the rest of your life. There is never a time when your education is unnecessary. Education is respected, and sometimes education is used to discriminate. While this is uncomfortable, it is true.

Now that you realized how important education is, it is time to make some changes. Brown vs. The Board of Education outlines how critical education is. Between financial investment and the legal tenure and other exhaustive measures, education is important! While it may not be fair, we are judged by our education. Even though, the available mechanisms are not always readily seen and available, we are still responsible for our own education, and particularly that of our children. Just as an example, you may have been reluctant about the need for this book. However, the value of the material has far outweighed the cost and time you have used to read it. By the reading of this book, you have determined that education is important. Likewise, you have decided that education is important enough to change your behavior and your attitude about education.

## A Family's Guide for Success

Because you have changed your approach, including your conversation about education, so have those around you. This is the posture that will lead to our overall success.

The posture you assume now is incredibly important because we are ineffective if we wait until after a failure to adjust our posture. We have to define education as important while we still have the student's attention, they are somewhat motivated, and we still have influence overall. We have to decide to be prominent and influential NOW! There is a distinct and unique opportunity by which we have to alter and direct the course of our children to personal, unprecedented excellence!

Let us take the opportunity to see what the value of it is.

Education is like travel. GPS became necessary for many Americans over the last decade. This GPS device gives turn by turn directions to a pre-selected destination. Whether you wanted to go or not, you were going, and you did not want to get lost. GPS ensures that you take the most direct route so that you are on time and safe. GPS also reroutes you when take a wrong turn.

This book and other resources, inclusive of the student's teacher, serve as GPS for educational success. The most important part of this plan is to decide to be successful. By the fact that you are holding this book, you may

## ARE YOU READY FOR 9ᵀᴴ GRADE... AGAIN?

have decided to be successful. Assuming that success is the goal, we may also assume that education is important to you.

In preparation for this book, several people were surveyed. None of them said they had the exact high school experience they should have. They all, however said that they would do high school differently, and even college, if they could do it all again. Those surveyed admitted that they would share with their children their experience to insure that their behavior was not repeated. The time for the importance of education is NOW! Wake up the whole family and let them all know that the next 1461 days (4 years with one certainly being a leap year) are serious and everybody needs to be present, focused, diligent, and energized! It is going to require all of us for the success to materialize the way we dreamed!

**I Would Rather Have It and Not Need It Than to Need It and Not Have It**

This old adage has applied in hundreds of thousands of situations; you may have never considered that it would apply to education. Education is needed and necessary at all times. The part of this that is critical is to "need it and not have it." It is difficult to read a job posting which contains education requirements that could eliminate your otherwise experienced resume from consideration.

## A Family's Guide for Success

In the nature of this economic climate and the pursuit of achievement with regard to the competitive nature of the various industries, education has changed the nature of the world. The requirements have increased to the point where a college degree is viewed as minimal. The exact phase that led to this is that having a bachelor's degree is just like have a high school diploma. This statement suggests two details: (1) everyone has a high school diploma, and (2) that a bachelor's degree has become so common that it is not enough of a distinguishing detail. The high school is not enough, so not having one is not optional.

What this statement overlooks is that both of those milestones are harder to accomplish for some. These are the years that are critical in our healthy life for our successful future.

Our goal is to have it when we need it so that we cancel any related disappointment if we did not have that required and highly coveted, 8" X 11," 80-lb sheet of paper that says we have successfully attended and passed all of the required courses as mandated by the national and state boards of education.

### The Employer Who Evaluates Education

Macy's is a major retailer. This retailer has merged with and taken over some of the best retailers ever created. Macy's has consumed an immense amount of market share and has gained a competitive edge by consuming and

## ARE YOU READY FOR 9TH GRADE... AGAIN?

eliminating nearly all of its competition. In the meantime, the Human Resources process has evolved several times within these transitions.

Macy's has a test that accompanies the lengthy application. This test asks a myriad of questions ranging from synonyms to mathematical reasoning problems. Further, the test is timed. This test is designed to measure your logical intellect and any reasoning that would lead to insight into your decision-making abilities. This test is graded and assessed by a computer based results generator that shares with the team if the applicant is the best fit for the company.

The test most surprised the author with the detailed math problems and the intense language arts scenarios. A friend of the author and the author were immediately alarmed about how this would affect the young people who would apply for a position with the company. We were convinced that they are unprepared for such exams. While we were not sure about how other retailers handled this scenario, we are certain that this will be a distinctively separating factor during the employment process.

While what Macy's has done is not illegal nor discriminatory, this was an alert for us to understand that the bar is being raised and the standards need to be recognized so that our students can be prepared to match and exceed those standards.

## A FAMILY'S GUIDE FOR SUCCESS

Education is everywhere, and it shows up in some unexpected methods. We are designed to help them prepare.

### Who Determines the Value of that Education?

The aggregate maximum loan amount in 2012 is $138,000. This means that a student can borrow $138,000 for her entire education in her lifetime (studentloans.gov). Based on the amount of the loans a student can borrow, the student can effectively owe more for her education than she owes for her home or her car. This monetary investment indicates the worth and value of education. This could be half of all your debt if you owed for a car and a $100,000 house.

We put the value of homes and cars on the same level with the value of education. Two of the three are long-term investments. The education is for your lifetime. The house could be for your lifetime. The car is unlikely to last nearly that long. While the education cannot technically be passed on, the legacy for earning an education can be passed on. That behavior creates a generational movement for education. The best stories are those grown-ups who share that they grew up with a history of educated family which left them no choice except to pursue education if they wanted to live in that family. The family sets the standard and expectation, with neither exception nor excuse for education. This expectation also promotes a belonging in the family so that it is

## Are You Ready for 9th Grade ... Again?

accomplished by a certain amount of pride that is welcomed by the family in order to carry on the family tradition.

Education occupies 25% of governmental discussions and funding. Many gimmicks have been voted into law in order to fund education. The lottery was made legal in some states with the express purpose to fund education. The states' constituents do not know if indeed those lofty funds are funding education as was promised.

We are certain that educational funding was cut severely between 2008 and 2012, affecting the teacher's salaries, books, transportation, and other essential details for a school, inclusive of technology.

Our students cannot afford those cuts or inconsistencies within education. Our students need a different kind of leadership regarding an explanation of the importance of education and how we are going to achieve such excellence with less: fewer resources and fewer persons who are as committed as your educators were.

Our students are going to develop their definition of importance based on how we treat the educators, parents, legislators and community leaders.

A student defines the importance of education by the time the stakeholders spend on education: both the time and money, but mostly by time. A student knows two details: when you are not prepared and when you do not

## A Family's Guide for Success

care. Children like time – your time and your undivided attention. They like it when we are prepared with our lessons and our expectations. We cannot manage them on the fly or based on other situations.

As parents, time and preparation mean that we need to be present for homework, reading and studying. If we are not able to help with problems, we need to secure a tutor and a plan for overcoming all related obstacles.

The teacher needs to be prepared to share with excellence the lesson and couple those lessons with compassion and genuine investment in their lives. This investment means time with listening, understanding, attending games where they are on the roster, and rewarding the students for the great effort and realized success.

Legislators are a little more distant however still the highest accountable. The changes that governments make impact billions of children for various periods of times. These are not, usually, easy to implement or reverse or modify. The costs of these changes are also incredibly impactful on the overall budget which further decreases the available resources which were already initially minimal. Legislators are not always mindful that while their children and grandchildren may not be affected by these movements, there are millions of children who are affected who are the children and grandchildren of millions of voters. Legislators, please legislate as if they come home with you every evening. Please legislate so that our educational system is respectable and is

## Are You Ready for 9th Grade... Again?

representative of the world super power we are when we wage war on others who do not behave as we would or as we would prescribe.

The community at-large needs to remember how to encourage and support our children in their efforts through tutoring, financial contributions and other voluntary efforts which propel their education forward with a fervency that we all can be proud of and to which we look forward.

## Why is Our Education Important?

Our education impacts our future, our self-image, our self-esteem and our opportunities. Our future is connected to our education. We also make decisions based on that education. We feel the freedom to pursue all of our options with the education we are afforded.

It is important because it is an opportunity that we are all afforded.

## Who Determines Its Worth?

The student determines how important that education is. The worth of the education depends on how the student regards that education, how they desire to use that education and how eagerly, and urgently they pursue their education. The student determines the worth of her education. If she values her education, then she will actively participate in her education by completing all classwork and homework assignments, complete reading assignments,

# A Family's Guide for Success

participating in classroom discussions, taking copious notes during class lectures, and asking for help as needed. The student will participate with a cooperative attitude about learning and will understand that her approach to her education will be matched, however not ever exceeded, by the stakeholders. She will only be helped further if she is heavily invested in her own education. Anything less than active participation will deem her lazy as a student and uninterested in what education provides. The only way to counter that is to participate actively in her education. Consistently.

The student determines the worth and value of this education. The student determines the future uses of this education. We cannot make the student learn or retain or seek knowledge. We can only present it and pray that she catches the vision we have for her and adopt it as her own. We have to be prepared if she does not feel the same way. She has to work to insure that she does pursue the excellence of education.

This may be a surprise yet it is time. The student offers value to education in such a manner that no one can parallel their experiences. Each child and experience are different.

Our job is to insure how to make that decision properly and keep the path toward successful achievement via education available and within reach with powerful expectations.

### Are You Ready for 9th Grade... Again?

> "I KNOW FROM MY OWN EDUCATION THAT IF I HADN'T ENCOUNTERED TWO OR THREE INDIVIDUALS THAT SPENT EXTRA TIME WITH ME, I'M SURE I WOULD HAVE BEEN IN JAIL."
>
> STEVE JOBS

**A FAMILY'S GUIDE FOR SUCCESS**

Are You Ready for 9th Grade... Again?

# Educational vs. Emotional

**7th Grade Math**

Math requires practice. Practice is defined as homework. Homework is designed to reinforce and remind the student of what they learned that day or any day. Homework is not seen of value or treated with any worth anymore. One morning the math teacher asked for her student's homework. Several students did not have their assignments. The teacher demanded that the students who did not have their homework to call their parents so that the parents would participate in their education. The call offended one parent to the point that she asked for a parent-teacher conference.

During the parent-teacher-student conference, the parent came to the conference with a defensive posture regarding her son and his performance. The parent did not own the fact that her child was failing because he was not participating and was not engaged in his education. The student was consumed with the lack of emotional attachment between him and the teacher rather than understanding the nature of the education that was before him.

During the conference, the parent does not ask her son why his assignments are blank. Nor does the mother seem concerned that he has decided to reject his education. She contributes and enables him in that she inappropriately supports his faulty reasoning regarding his response to the teacher.

When a student decides that the is not going to do the work, the student is saying that she is no longer participating, and she does not desire to learn. When she is decisive enough no to learn, this behavior is indicative of greater issues. These issues need to be resolved so that we can educate your kids. We cannot afford the emotional shut down your child has staged as a means for getting our attention. During that emotional shut down, you have missed valuable instruction that cannot be repeated or recovered. At this point, your child is frustrated and now is failing.

The 7th grader then goes on to reveal to the teacher that he does not hate her. The teacher shares that she does not care whether he likes her or not. His education should be more important than whether he likes and has a personal relationship with the teacher.

The student and the parent are both under the false impression that this matters to move toward a successful education. Further, the parent shares that the teacher and the student have a personality conflict. These two areas are dangerous in that this introduces confusion to the otherwise objective educational environment. The teacher is firm in her approach and assures that none of his personal feelings matter because in math, personality does not matter while grading. Math is objective, so grading is objective and straight forward.

## ARE YOU READY FOR 9ᵀᴴ GRADE ... AGAIN?

Again, the parent does not embrace the fact the student has made a poor choice to not participate in his education.

We have to steer our students away from the emotional response that so easily is misunderstood as important in how we are educated. The parent needs to be engaged at a higher level.

The 7th grader was eventually changed to another educator, and he still failed the class. This further supports our objective of education. The parent and the student were focused on the wrong thing. Our students need DIRECTION regarding remaining focused on the education at hand. Otherwise, we will waste a lot of time and energy on matters unrelated to education.

**Get Yours, I Got Mine**

This adage is one which is inappropriately used to spark some urgency within the hearts of the children. The question is 'are we really inspiring the student' when we use this phrase. Not necessarily. The phrase has quite the opposite effect.

We may consider sharing our stories in such a manner that moves our young people toward excellence. The intention of the statement has been misunderstood and not well received. This does not move us closer to the goal of an educated generation.

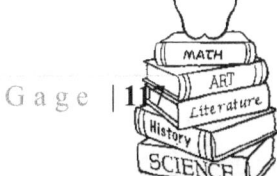

## A Family's Guide for Success

When you share the story, please give the important details. These details include how long it took for you to graduate, how hard it was to graduate, what happened as a result of your graduation, what you regret most about your attention toward your education, and what you wish you had done differently while in school. You could include how if certain details had been different then, college entrance would have been better.

Tell them enough to entice them to give their best at school, understanding that no one is perfect; we have all made mistakes, yet we have recovered and done well.

The objective is to instill hope for an otherwise bleak forecast in our student's future. Educators and parents, please handle our students carefully in this area.

### Alphabetically Speaking

Education comes before emotion even in the dictionary. Likewise, education should come before emotion in the classroom and at home. Keep in mind our children adopt our disposition, whether we intend for them to or not. Your children are a reflection of you. They talk and gesture based on how you talk and gesture. The most important part is the emotion, and the emotional response is a characteristic they, usually, adopt from you. Keep in mind that when you respond with words, "red" ones, those words may be repeated, and

## ARE YOU READY FOR 9TH GRADE... AGAIN?

they are ALWAYS repeated in an embarrassing situation. As parents, we need to monitor our reactions. Our children use those reactions to create their mindset and behavior.

One student mentioned once that her mother was not going to care about her attire and her grades. She mentioned this indignantly and authoritatively as if she had heard those words from her parent. The problem was the mother probably never intended for that to be repeated. There are emotions that should be kept out of the eyes and ears of your children so that we do not have to defend some of those unfortunate statements you never intended to be repeated.

We are emotional about our children, as we should be. However, we need to be clear that their education is paramount. Please figure out how to manage your feelings, as well as teach your children how to do the same. The children need your maturity. Likewise, we need to seek to understand what the outcome needs to be versus what we are hearing from our children. This is a time to speak candidly to our children about the successful path we have mentally designed.

Realize that our children's education is necessary. We cannot interrupt that with some misplaced emotions and risk shutting down the educational process. These remarks may seem repetitive, however, it is concerning when

# A FAMILY'S GUIDE FOR SUCCESS

parents allow students to ignore the main reason why they are in school: to leave equipped for the world at large and all of its expectations and contents.

We can better manage those emotions by remembering to communicate with the teacher and your student what is needed to succeed, keeping the goal front and center, and training the educational experience in such a manner that they both understand you are not moved but minor obstacles.

If you keep it in order, then they both will as well.

**Education Comes Before Emotion Even in the Dictionary.**

How do we manage to get so emotional? How do we get so emotional when our child is WRONG? The only person who is hurt when this happens is the child. The student at the conference was invested in liking or not liking the teacher. Because he did not like her, he opted out of doing his work. Who really lost in this scenario? When the student made that choice, he hurt himself. The problem is that the parent did not visit about his lack of engagement and participation but about whether they had a personality conflict. Children and adults do not have personality conflicts. The teacher who knows that knows that the parent and the student have low educational priorities and a false sense of reality. This knowledge affects how the teacher addresses the student and his education.

## Are You Ready for 9th Grade... Again?

Whether we agree or not, the educator has tried to engage the student, and hold him accountable much to no avail. With so much demand on her time, she does not have time to demand a fertile location to invest her time of him while she sacrifices the opportunity to educate her other thirty students in that class, of her 180 for the day. So who really loses?

The teacher weighs her opportunity cost of begging someone to learn when she is surrounded with at least two dozen other eager minds. The time she spent begging no longer seems appealing.

Last note, the parent and the teacher are assumed to have the same objective, however when this is non-congruent, and there is a clear disconnect for the objective, it becomes even easier to work with cooperative, and engaged parents. Remember sometimes our emotional response can cost ourselves and our students.

Education comes before emotion in the dictionary. It is hard to do but with so many other needs and demands, the teacher attends to those who have a definite focus on education and realize it is not necessary to like the teacher in order to learn. Just as a side note, the parent never mentioned the teacher's teaching style or the speed of her delivery or the pace of her lessons or the amount of homework expected or the rigor of the instruction. Those are the reasons why pedagogy exists. These are the factors of great lessons and further,

## A Family's Guide for Success

great classroom experiences. Those are the characteristics of an awesome educator.

### ARE YOU READY FOR 9TH GRADE... AGAIN?

"I'M A VERY BIG BELIEVER IN EQUAL OPPORTUNITY AS OPPOSED TO EQUAL OUTCOME. EQUAL OPPORTUNITY TO ME, MORE THAN ANYTHING, MEANS A GREAT EDUCATION. MAYBE EVEN MORE IMPORTANT THAN A GREAT FAMILY LIFE. WE COULD MAKE SURE THAT EVERY YOUNG CHILD IN THIS COUNTRY GOT A GREAT EDUCATION. WE FALL FAR SHORT OF THAT."

STEVE JOBS

**A FAMILY'S GUIDE FOR SUCCESS**

ARE YOU READY FOR 9ᵀᴴ GRADE... AGAIN?

# Motivating Your 9th Grader

**Listening to Your 9th Grader**

Are you listening to your 9th grader? What is your 9th grader saying to you? Are you hearing what she is saying? What are her concerns? Are those concerns being addressed? Are her needs being met? Is the education she is experiencing beneficial to the student?

What is causing you to listen? What kinds of details are you listening for in your conversation with your child? What questions should you ask your 9th grader?

As you listen to your children, you are listening for engagement and excitement. You are listening for high levels of interest and a complete understanding. You are listening for eagerness in the learning process. You are listening for hope and promise. You are listening for a spirit of excellence. Here are the questions we need to ask:

- Do you like school?

- Why/why not?

- What is your favorite subject? Why?

# A FAMILY'S GUIDE FOR SUCCESS

- What is your least favorite subject? Why?

- Who is your favorite teacher? Why?

- Who is your all-time favorite teacher? Why?

- What keeps you motivated to go to school? Why?

- Do you understand the value of education?

- Do you understand the opportunities education affords you?

- Who is your example that education is important?

- What do you plan to do with your education?

- Where do you plan to attend college?

- What do you intend to major in?

- What career will you pursue first?

- How did you learn to manage your time?

- Do you need more help with your time management?

- Do you need help with your study skills?

- How did you learn how to study?

## ARE YOU READY FOR 9TH GRADE... AGAIN?

- How do you handle frustration when you are having difficulty grasping the concept?

- Who helps you when you have difficulty with the concept(s)?

- What subject requires the most effort from you?

- What subject requires the least effort from you?

- How do you learn?

- How do you handle personal conflict at school?

- Do you know your counselor?

- Do you feel comfortable approaching your counselor about anything you need?

- What teachers compliment you when you do well?

- What kind of reward system do you need to keep you excited about the education?

- What do you do to stay focused in class?

- Do you do your homework? If so, 100%, 75%, 25%, 10%? Do you complete it, even if you do not know for sure the answer?

## A Family's Guide for Success

- Do you understand why homework is necessary? Do you view homework as practice?

- Do you get nervous when reading in front of the class?

- Do you have influence with your friends to motivate them to do their best?

- Do you wish for others to be educated too?

Now that you are aware of what to ask, you have to remember to listen. This may be difficult, but you need to let your student know you are attentive to her needs. Do not interrupt when he is explaining. Give credit for the world they have at their fingertips. Give credit for sound judgment and wise counsel within your child. Let her present her failures and her successes. Listen to the details she discloses.

### Believing

Believing in herself is the start of confidence. Believing in her is worth gold. If she knows that you believe in her, she will keep trying, and she will remain focused. As the parent, you think that she already knows that I believe in her. She should already know because I do _____, _____, and _____, _____, and _____. Those blanks represent what you do and buy and think and feel. One mother used to say if it were not for her child she could live under the bridge. What she was trying to express is that she did what

## Are You Ready for 9th Grade... Again?

she did because of her love, care and concern. The problem is that the daughter does not measure love that same way the mother does.

THE CHILD NEEDS TO HEAR THAT YOU BELIEVE. Children do not apply belief, or love for that matter, in an abstract matter the way we have grown to do. Tell her, and tell her often. Remember you are the stable factor and the positive reinforcement in her life. You are her solution to whatever happens in the outside world. You have to believe, and she has to know you believe in her. Belief is consistent. Belief is powerful. Belief is empowering. Belief is non-judgmental. Belief stirs hope. Belief starts with a promise. Believing in your child regardless of his track record and attitude and knowledge is what he is waiting on to be successful. Believing is contagious.

### Asking

Our average teenager has an attitude. Yes, they do. You have to ask the questions. The questions are designed to deepen and increase your dialogue with your teenager.

- How do you feel about yourself?

- Who are your friends? When will I meet them?

- What is your definition of a friend?

- What are your goals?

# A FAMILY'S GUIDE FOR SUCCESS

- What do I do that you admire?

- Who are your other role models?

- When will you have sex?

- How do you determine with whom to have sex?

- Do you feel empowered to make good decisions?

- How do you make decisions? What process do you use?

- What excites you?

- What motivates you?

- Who are your friend's parents?

- Where do you want to go to college?

- Why do you want to go to college?

- What's the best part of your day?

- How do you define love?

- Who loves you?

- Whom do you love?

## ARE YOU READY FOR 9ᵀᴴ GRADE ... AGAIN?

- What causes you not to forgive?

These questions represent a sample set of the questions you need to ask your teenager. These questions are essential for the dialogue with your teenager. This relationship needs constant growth and facilitation. Knowledge is your job.

- What do you think about drugs?

- Will you try drugs?

- What will it take for you to say no?

- What do you feel about alcohol?

- Will you consume alcohol?

- What will it take for you to say no?

- Would you pose for nude photos?

- Would you send pictures of yourself to another person?

Use these answers to grow a powerful relationship.

**Supporting**

Support defines comprehensive parenting. You are his leader, and your support is not optional, nor random. Support is attending games, knowing the rules and wearing his jersey/number. Support is going to her plays and

# A FAMILY'S GUIDE FOR SUCCESS

musicals, remembering when she changes friends and understanding what motivates her.

Support happens up close – not from a distance. Support has evolved over the years. With the ever changing technology, support can be in the form of a text message and an email; you can tweet and other social media. Your support is invaluable to your child's success. Educators can tell when a child does not have the support of her parents. The lack of support shows in her attitude and sometimes, his grades and most often in their behavior.

Support needs to happen consistently. Support has to happen daily. Without fail! They believe what they see, not what they hear. This support has to happen daily and needs to be blatantly obvious to the child daily. There can be no assumption of your support.

Support needs to happen proactively. Proactive constitutes deliberate support. Find ways to support your student. Regular emails to the teachers about what your student needs. Keep in mind that your student needs to understand the value of their efforts. This is a great time to share college information with your students. College applications need to be considered. College tours should be on the travel schedule.

Support requires transparency. There will be times when you have to share what kind of student you were and what kind of student you hope your

## ARE YOU READY FOR 9ᵀᴴ GRADE ... AGAIN?

child will be/become. Tell her why you are concerned and why you are present. Tell her how you feel when you cannot do the homework. Then find someone who does know how. Go to school early or late one day to the tutorials yourself and ask the teacher for help. This interaction will affirm your child so that your child feels better about asking questions. She needs to be able to ask questions and not feel "dumb."

Support is non-transferable. Nobody can support your child in your place. You are the only person who can support your child like you are supposed to and can support her.

## The Backpack

The key to success is in the backpack. As one parent discovered, searching the backpack regularly will help you in several ways. Inspection of the backpack will insure that the student is completing all assignments. Likewise, if the student knows that you are inspecting, rather than just asking about the assignments, she is more likely not to lie about completing their work. High school assumes that the training that was instilled in elementary school is still in place, which could not be any further from the truth. You got out of the habit of signing the agenda and the reading log the day your student was promoted to sixth grade. The problem is that the accountability also stopped. The student needs more accountability, not less. The sixth through twelfth

## A Family's Guide for Success

grades are all about change and empowerment and courage. This is a critical time. This is the path of preparation for the real world.

The backpack represents that preparedness for the rest of their lives. The maintenance of their regular life is your parental report card. The educators judge your child's future by the completion of the assignments, attitude and behavior. The educator judges you similarly as your child is an extension of you. There is no reason that you and your child are not alike.

The backpack is a level of accountability that needs to remain intact so that we can be successful.

### Rewards

We as adults reward ourselves all the time, sometimes for no reason at all. How do we reward our children? Is it based on some practical process which is consistent and aligned with his performance?

We need to reconsider simply giving the newest phone or gadgets just because we can afford it, or they asked for it. Rather we need to attach those gifts as rewards for great grades and awesome behavior.

These rewards give our students something to work for and look forward to. Share these rewards with the teacher so that this partnership can be mutually beneficial and with a weighted accountability.

### ARE YOU READY FOR 9ᵀᴴ GRADE... AGAIN?

**Technology-Systems (The Grade Book)**

Technology has taken over the grade book. You can view your child's grades online. You can monitor your child's progress. With this ability, you can do a strategic move. This move is best-shared as an example.

If your child has an 88, you can introduce the concept of asking what work is required to earn the two-grade points needed to earn a 90, an A. This can be taught and mastered. When you show your child how to seek this information, then you are empowering them to seek her own best.

This starts with showing him how to check the grades, determine the goal, understand how to achieve the goal, and how to ask for the goal. We need to teach our students how to negotiate for what they need. This conversation is the start of life coaching.

Use this to your advantage and to that of your child.

**Visiting the Campus – SURPRISE**

The campus visit is essential! While your child has not invited you to her school in a few years, she still does excite when you bring her lunch or drop her jacket at the school.

## A Family's Guide for Success

This visit also could comprise of a class sit-in. A visit to the career, college and guidance counselors could also fit into this visit. Keep in mind that this is your job.

The other outcome of this visit is to surprise your child. Why would you do that, you may be thinking. The surprise serves many purposes, one of which is to let your child know that you can show up at any time. He needs to know that this is possible. There are outstanding accountability and respect associated with this. Likewise, this surprise also exhibits to the team of educators and administrators that you are serious about your child's education.

Educators and children behave differently when parents are visible, knowledgeable and educated about the process of education. Your visits assert some of that advocacy. Consider these regular surprise visits as part of your routine and keep the school and district policies handy.

Also, consider volunteering on a regular basis. The PTO/PTA needs your presence as well. Please seek opportunities to make your presence known and your contribution of the overall enhancement of the school.

## Are You Ready for 9ᵀᴴ Grade... Again?

"EDUCATION COMES BEFORE EMOTION, EVEN IN THE DICTIONARY. YOUR EDUCATION IS FAR MORE IMPORTANT THAN HOW YOU FEEL. PLEASE DO NOT LET YOUR FEELINGS STIFLE YOUR EDUCATION."

ONEDIA N. GAGE

**A FAMILY'S GUIDE FOR SUCCESS**

ARE YOU READY FOR 9ᵀᴴ GRADE... AGAIN?

# Parent-Teacher-Student Conference/Communication

The parent-teacher conference is the source of solutions, conflict resolutions, and affirmations. This conference is designated to solve problems, create a good working relationship and understand the needs of the involved parties. The parent-teacher conference needs to be handled in a professional, advocacy manner.

The parties involved are the teacher, the parent, and the student. The educator or teacher, sometimes includes the counselor and an administrator depending on the nature of the conference, is there for the instructional leadership. The parent is there as the responsible party and advocate. The student is the person who is responsible for the work and action.

The conference outcome is designed to offer support and come to an agreement about what the parties need to accomplish and how those goals will be accomplished.

**Do**

The new parent-teacher-student conference should include what we are going to do. This is about action – not blame. Someone is to blame for each

## A Family's Guide for Success

issue we discuss. In the parent-teacher-student conference, we are solving the issues. Do be proactive about the previous and potential issues. Do move aggressively toward solutions. Part of this urgency will mean that we share those issues and immediately implement the solution. Likewise, we do need to be honest about what is actually occurring.

Do put your guard down. Please keep the conversation focused on facts. This conference is limited regarding emotions. This objectivity will keep us all focused on the student's education.

Share what is relevant to your child's education with the educator. This sharing includes any medical issues, medication, family dynamics, recent life changing events, educational concerns, and previous educational successes and failures. These details help the educator judge how to help your student.

There are times when these details are shared so the student has a better chance to be successful. Often the details we need as educators are not shared until it is presented as an excuse. After a total disruption of the classroom, the lunchroom, and the school, sharing with the team of educators that your son has ADHD or that his grandmother has just died or that your family is now homeless is too late to be received well. These pieces of information are important as they happen to your student and your family. This information is held confidentially but is useful for managing your child and his emotions. We use this information to understand your child's attitude and disposition.

### ARE YOU READY FOR 9ᵀᴴ GRADE . . . AGAIN?

You might be considering what to do with that information differently if you did not have it. Well, here is what the difference is: when you know someone is hungry but you are trying to teach them but because they are hungry, they cannot hear you or learn anything. This information is the source of his distraction. We need to know how to feed them so that he can pay attention in class.

The sharing reminds us to be compassionate to others and introduces us to the thoughts and needs of that child. Sharing may cause your educators to reach out and research for you to overcome those circumstances. We all fall into the "box" of do not tell others what we are experiencing. However, we need each other in this scenario. These life changing events affect our children differently than they do us so when they experience challenge, their response to challenge manifests itself in many different ways, which are often detrimental and irreversible.

Children request our attention through their behavior. They often use their behavior, attitude and grades to get your UNDIVIDED attention!

They are not able to articulate all that in their conversation. They do not even know where or how to start and who will listen to them. Sharing is valuable. Do it. Teachers discover meaningful information within the confines of a conference.

## A Family's Guide for Success

This is an excellent time to share how you feel. These feelings are important because those feelings impact actions and behaviors and thoughts. Remember that emotions and feelings need to be managed and not allowed to cloud over our better judgment on how to handle our children.

This is also a time to hear from all parties! Active listening is required. All persons in the room have a voice that needs to be respected and given the appropriate weight for the complete message. You are listening for answers to your questions and concerns.

Ask all of the questions. Do not leave anything out. ASK. Ask until everything is resolved.

Stephen Covey in the 7 Habits of Highly Effective People states that we should seek first to understand others before being understood. Are you trying to understand the other people in the room? Maybe not. Based on the fact that you are compelled by your child to be here, it is wise to understand her needs, issues and fears. It is time to understand what she needs to do to be successful. In this understanding, you may also be doing some translating.

**Building Bridges**

Use this conference to build a bridge with your educator team. You need to develop relationships with her teachers because you need eyes, ears and

## Are You Ready for 9th Grade... Again?

advocates on campus. A village is required to educate a child. A TEAM. You need this bridge for you and your child to crossover.

Educators will need to write recommendation letters. They also have access to information that you need for your child. They are the advisors for the extracurricular activities your child needs for college applications and well-roundedness.

Finally, cooperating in the parent-teacher-student conference is the best approach. If or when your child is failing or at a critical point, these educators share with your child how to succeed, as well as with you. These are essential relationships. You need them to help you educate your child. They impart character and work ethic. They share wit and wisdom. All of this is based on relationship.

## The Begging Session

David's mother arrived at the parent-teacher-student conference with a notepad and a smile. She was ready to take notes and ask questions. She arrived with the attitude of this meeting was called to "save" my son even if it is from himself. After the introductions had been made around the room, Mom spoke first. She opened with a profoundly unexpected commentary, where she offered her sincerest apologies for her son's lack of work ethic and overall engagement. At that point, she had a room on the edge of their seats.

# A FAMILY'S GUIDE FOR SUCCESS

Mom further questioned each educator with the same questions. What does my son need to complete in order to pass your class? What is his conduct like in your class? Her poise and overall disposition were unlike any other conference ever. She did not seek to blame the educators. She took notes on everything that was said about his work. After the second teacher had shared, the other teachers seemed to relax the requirements as well as offering additional methods to recover his grade. As the compassion and benevolence in the room increased, there was a camaraderie that was developing in the room.

During the session, she comments, "I know that this is a begging session. I know that you all do not have to do any of this for my son." This statement caused a hush to blanket the room. Again the stakeholders increased their investment in the student. One teacher answered that his grade would be an "I." The "I" will be replaced with the next grading cycle's grade. The educator went on to say that he had a mound of work ahead and did not want him to become overwhelmed and, as a result, quit.

Mom's attitude was unprecedented. She controlled the entire meeting and held the hearts and minds of the educators in the palm of her hand. She was honest, sincere, and humble.

Her son completed his work with everyone's help. He never let his grades fall again. She never had to visit under the same circumstances again.

## Are You Ready for 9th Grade . . . Again?

He learned a lot, especially about the love of his mom for him. It took great courage to come and be that mom in front of all them and in front of her son.

Mom admitted her own shortcomings while making promises that she kept. Her stand was remarkable and moving. She inspired an entire team on the behalf of her son.

### Do NOT Embarrass Me

In the 1970's, corporal punishment was permitted at schools, at least in Texas. In Houston, Texas, there was a precocious student who was intelligent and talkative. The child's parent had a "don't embarrass me" policy. This policy carried her well into her life. This policy included that if the child was in trouble or that a school visit was required, the WHOLE STORY needed to be shard at home before the conference was held. This meant FULL DISCLOSURE was required – no matter how bad it may appear to be.

The opposite was to let her parents find out in the meeting what really happened. This is embarrassing to the parent. Her mother would rather the worst of it at home, so that she could be mentally and emotionally prepared, rather than informed in front of the educators/administrators.

That child became an educator and now shares that same principle to all students. The student needs to be coached on how to share the bad news. Likewise, as parents we need to not embarrass our students. They have to live

# A Family's Guide for Success

with the scene you caused until they leave the school. You do not want to be known as the parent who is "crazy" or "lacks self-control" or the parent everyone hides from. You do not want your child to have to endure that label.

Mutual respect and honor are required.

## The Child Advocate

Briana was upset and decided not to do her work. She has decided not to participate in class and does not do her homework. She is obstinate to her teachers. She is mean and rude. She is unloving and unlovable. She is beautiful but does not know it, and when someone tells her that she is beautiful, she does not believe them. She is disruptive in class. She is disrespectful to her teachers. She interrupts the education of the other students. Her teachers demand a conference. This conference was held with the student's uncle.

Around the table, the looks are fierce. The educators are positioned for attack. As the conference starts, the revelation was made. This announcement made one educator stand in as an advocate. This announcement explained everything that had transpired to date. The counselor announced that Briana's mother died earlier in the year. The educator, now advocate, took charge of the meeting in a sweeping manner by redirecting her colleagues away from their anger and disdain.

## ARE YOU READY FOR 9™ GRADE ... AGAIN?

Between her pointed questions of both the student and the teacher, the educator brokered several agreements for the student and the team. This information included a discipline plan for when her thoughts and feelings overwhelm her.

No one at the table could empathize with the student. Briana was angry, and she had a great reason. This conversation should have happened at the start of the school year. Further, the uncle never spoke in the conference. Briana took a defiant attitude about life and school. However, after this conference, she was engaged in her work, she was successful and she graduated on time.

Every conference needs an advocate. Sometimes it is you. Sometimes it is someone else.

## On Two Sides of the Same Story Even When Worldly Different

Dante missed the scheduled parent-teacher-student conference. His side of the story was that he wants to do better but does not know how. His mother states that he does not take his education seriously. The team spent time talking to her about how to help her son be successful. Mom was surprised about the team's perspective of her son. She did not see what they saw. Daily. The team enlightened her on his approach to education. They shared his personal relationships and how he socialized with others.

# A Family's Guide for Success

She realized that she did not know enough about her child. She took the information seriously as well as questions about how he progressed.

She was encouraged by the genuine feedback. One team member specifically told mom to go home and hug her son. She was surprised to hear her son was a great young man who likes constant attention and needs constant affirmation.

This encouragement was not what she expected. She stated as much. She further stated that she would take the advice of the team.

Even though he was not there, his behavior improved, and so did his grades. The conference was successful.

## Seek to Understand the Heart of the Educator

The heart of the educator is a tender, harmonious spot for children who need education and an advocate. The educator wants the child to want to learn. She does not want to have beg the student to learn or to retain information. Most educators love their jobs. They find their influence over kids their duty.

As a parent, try to see your child through her lens. Your child's educator can see the application of the actual potential of your child. The educator sees things in your child that you have always hoped for but did not know were actually embedded within her. The educator sees your child for

## Are You Ready for 9th Grade... Again?

eight hours each day, doing things and talking to other students that you will never know.

Trust the heart of that educator unless you have factual evidence otherwise. That means a voice recording of her saying "I hate your child." Otherwise, TRUST!

The heart of the educator is not complicated to discern. The heart considers children and their value to our future. Also, realize that educators meet 200 new students each year, with an incoming class size of 1000. As they meet new students, they naturally seek out the best for them. The educator expects for that student and his parents to be on the same page.

Educators desire to breed a new generation of overcomers, dreamers, achievers, and successors. This cannot happen without the consent, commitment, and cooperation of all parties.

The heart of the educator is mostly pure. How did we reach that conclusion? An educator was most often a serious student and a good student. Real educators want the same for each of their students. They are offended when students do not diligently seek their own education.

The educator grades herself on how many students leave successful overall and how prepared they are for the future. The educator comes prepared to transform minds. The above average educator is eternally optimistic about

# A Family's Guide for Success

what her children can achieve. She is focused on enhancing the lives of your entire family. You will be amazed at what your child trusts her educator with – sometimes with more than she trusts with you.

Invest in your educator!

## Questions to Ask at the Conference

What can I do to help my child be successful?

What is her best subject?

What is her worst subject?

What kind of activities engage my child the most?

How do you motivate my student?

How can I motivate my child?

How can I help my child when I do not know the material?

What can I do to help my student be better prepared for class?

What are the supplies I need to send to school?

What supplies do I need to have at home?

How do I help my child stay focused?

# Are You Ready for 9th Grade... Again?

How can I help my child improve his academic performance?

How can I help my child make the best of her time?

How can I help my child improve his behavior? Without the medication?

How would you like me to communicate with you?

What is my role in my child's education?

May I visit your classroom to see how you present material?

May I visit your classroom to observe my child's classroom behavior?

May I have a copy of the assignments they are to complete each week?

How can I refresh/learn information that would help my child move forward?

Are there any enrichment programs or summer activities that I should enroll my child in?

How do you reward your students?

What areas should my child need to work on?

Is my child respectful?

Is my child attentive?

Is my child a hard worker?

## A Family's Guide for Success

Is my child easy to engage in class?

Does my child have smart friends?

Does he ask questions?

Does he remember information easily?

Does he work well in groups?

Does he have to be often redirected?

Is he well-liked by the other students and teachers?

When are tutorials?

**Communication Tips/Strategies**

Initial Contact:

- In person appointment made by phone or email

Follow-up Contact:

- Email: checking in, asking for progress, asking for specific clarification; it is appropriate to ask for an explanation and answer to any problem you and the student could not figure out. We highly recommend taking a picture of the problem and attaching it to the email.

## ARE YOU READY FOR 9ᵀᴴ GRADE... AGAIN?

- Phone: if you need to share some pertinent and personal information

- In person: based on behavior, grades and other areas of concern.

Please do not be defensive.

Please ask. Do not assume anything.

Remember that you are approaching an adult who may also be a parent.

Remember that you need them.

Be honest.

Be kind.

Be transparent.

**The Outcome & The Contract**

The outcome of a teacher-parent-student conference is a better work ethic and a more focused student. The outcome should be better grades, better attitude, better communication and a better understanding of what should be happening with your student and yourself.

As we leave the conference, the contract will stipulate the commitments of each party. This will include the completion of all assignments, satisfactory test scores, and the consequences of not doing those activities. This contract

## A Family's Guide for Success

will outline the communication contract and process. This contract will share the contents of the meeting.

All parties should sign and receive a copy of the contract. The contract should be reviewed bi-weekly so that we are sure that we are meeting the needs of the student and that your student is doing his part.

This contract affirms the importance of the education we hope that the student will pursue.

# Are You Ready for 9th Grade...Again?

"I BELIEVE THAT WE LEARN BY PRACTICE. WHETHER IT MEANS TO LEARN TO DANCE BY PRACTICING DANCING OR TO LEARN TO LIVE BY PRACTICING LIVING, THE PRINCIPLES ARE THE SAME. IN EACH, IT IS THE PERFORMANCE OF A DEDICATED PRECISE SET OF ACTS, PHYSICAL OR INTELLECTUAL, FROM WHICH COMES SHAPE OF ACHIEVEMENT, A SENSE OF ONE'S BEING, A SATISFACTION OF SPIRIT."

MARTHA GRAHAM

**A FAMILY'S GUIDE FOR SUCCESS**

ARE YOU READY FOR 9ᵀᴴ GRADE . . . AGAIN?

# The Student

**Voice**

Our students have a voice. A voice that sometimes we render silent. We require our children and students to be quiet when we should consider letting our students speak. We silence their voice because we do not believe or trust in what they will say. We do not trust their attitude or mind. We are not sure that we are going to like their perspective or view. We do not value their opinion. We are not interested in what they want. This is unfortunate!

Their voice is powerful and insightful! Their voice is transparent! Our students are prepared to share what is on their minds. They are thoughtful about more than we give them credit for. They need to practice those thoughts in front of us so that when they are out in the world they have the confidence to express themselves appropriately. The other purpose is to check their facts. The misinformation passed between teens based on the internet, television and rumors are rampant. The only way to know what they know is to hear what they have to say. They have to hear the words come out of their own mouths. We are there to advise and correct.

In the academic setting, their voice is important because this is the first real world situation when we can observe their decision-making skills. We have

## A Family's Guide for Success

to acknowledge that our students currently take in much more than we did at their age. Between the internet and the new commercial standard, our children are exposed to so much more than we were. They have more information to understand, and more importantly to filter. They also have to determine what can be used and repeated. Their academic voice is important because they need to understand what is being taught, why it is being taught, and how they will use this now and later. They need to be coached in their academic voice. You need to understand how to manage this process. Below are some of the concerns which should be addressed in the academic voice, which applies to both of you.

Does the educator care about children?

Does this educator care about my child?

How invested is the educator in my child's success?

How invested is my child in his/her own success?

What tools and resources are available to us for our success?

What does my child understand about this subject?

What does my child not understand about this subject?

What can be done to increase his/her understanding?

How do I enlist more help for my child?

## ARE YOU READY FOR 9ᵀᴴ GRADE ... AGAIN?

How do I follow up on my child's progress?

Is the educator aware of anything that may cause delayed learning?

Does my child know that she/he is responsible for his/her education?

Does my child know how to ask for help?

Would you please help me?

Would you please help my child?

Is my child doing his/her very best?

Is there anything I can do to insure my child's success?

Who is my child's advocate in this school?

How often do you communicate success and concerns?

How much technology do we have available to assist the success?

How engaged is my child in the learning process?

Does my child ask questions/participate in class?

      Likewise, the educator is going to share with you according to what is asked and expected of her/him. When we consider you and your child's voice, remember that certain emotions are inappropriate and misplaced. The child will get confused about an educator liking them. The child wants to be liked. While that may be important at some level, we need to remember that an educator may have 180 students or more each day. The educator's goal is not to like but educate each one. You and your child need to understand that "liking" and "caring" are different. Care is more important. Commitment to success is more important. 'Like' is superficial, possibly based on material influences.

Those are also emotional words. This is not an emotional relationship in high school. In elementary school, emotion was first. In high school, emotion is not on the list. The voice will be distorted if we are confused about what is important. Further, the educator will invest at the same level as you and your child – not any higher. Please do not expect the educator to do more for your child than your child, and you do. This is unreasonable.

One parent demanded that the educator do more than she was doing. She had not verified that her child had completed his assignments by looking in his backpack. Later, she discovered that he lied about completing his assignments. Then when she asked what else would be done for him. The educators shared when tutorials were offered. Her response was that he was attending driver's education classes when tutorials were offered.

When the parent chose driver's education, she silenced her campaign. The parent let everyone know that driving was more important than his

## ARE YOU READY FOR 9ᵀᴴ GRADE... AGAIN?

academic success. She sabotaged the child. The educator is not going to do anything extra.

In order for your voice to be heard and respected, you need to be 100% invested. Your child needs to seek the educator's investment by owning his/her responsibilities in the educational process.

These are some examples of what should happen:

- How many points away from an A am I?
- Do you offer extra credit?
- What do I need to work on to be better in this subject?
- Where did I go wrong on this assignment?
- What does it take to be successful?
- Are there some resources I can use to improve?
- What time and where are tutoring sessions?
- I have shown my work but seem to keep getting it wrong. Can you show me where I went wrong?

These all show investment and concern about a child's personal decision to learn. The child has to be reminded and coached to use his/her voice. That coaching is your job.

# A Family's Guide for Success

This voice is a key to the success of your child. The time you spend developing that voice is necessary for your success.

## Feelings

Your child has a specific set of feelings related to education and certain subjects in particular. These feelings can stifle the education process. It is important that they share their feelings with you and that you know how they feel. It is more important that they understand that their education is more important: paramount. We have to help them understand that when we allow or invite our feelings to override our education, we have made a HUGE mistake! Likewise, keeping these feelings and emotions in the proper perspective will allow us to focus on our education better.

Again, how we think that the educator feels about us is not important. How we decide to pursue our education with all the passion, zest, zeal and enthusiasm that we have and can borrow is what is critical and what you control. Focus on what you actually control; not what you wished you could control.

## Behavior

Our students need to honor the school rules and respect the educators. Poor behavior distracts from the educational environment. Further, the rules have changed since you graduated. Foul language earns your student a ticket that leads to court fees and court visits. Fighting can earn you a ticket and jail

## Are You Ready for 9th Grade... Again?

time. Further, recording the fight can be used to issue your children a ticket and can be used in a court of law. Are you surprised? It sure surprised others who have discovered the new policies.

Poor behavior is, usually, an indicator that your student needs attention. Attention could include conversation, time, hug, or/and praise. When you consider what you child needs to keep him/her encouraged, you need to remain in tune with your child. Poor behavior is designed to get our attention. However, poor behavior is unacceptable because it's disruptive, costly, time consuming and unnecessary.

Solving poor behavior is a challenge. There are tips following to assist with poor behavior.

1. Communication solves some of the expectations about behavior.

2. Understanding your child's trigger points. Share those points with your child's educators.

3. Keep in mind that you are ultimately responsible for their behavior. Financially and academically.

4. Poor behavior needs to be understood as a planned or spontaneous distraction of knowledge.

## A Family's Guide for Success

5. Help your child pursue the areas that offer the frustration in his/her education.

6. Remind your child that learning is the reason for coming to school.

7. Be consistent in discipline when poor behavior happens.

8. Seek to understand the issues that your child is having when poor behavior happens, and if that behavior is persistent.

9. Remind your child that you love him/her. Show him/her.

10. Ask how you can aid in better behavior on a consistent basis.

Be encouraged! Poor behavior is temporary and can be resolved. Stay focused and purposed!

**Attitude**

While there is not any certainty on how attitude develops, there are so many factors that contribute to the attitude. As parents, your job description includes shaping your child's attitude. This attitude, whether good or bad, drives our children's thoughts and achievements or lack thereof. Your attitude determines how much you let in. Likewise, your child's attitude will determine how much is offered to you and your child. People do "favors" for those persons that they like. You may be thinking that my child should be helped

## ARE YOU READY FOR 9TH GRADE... AGAIN?

regardless of whether she/he is liked. That is true. However, if your child has a poor attitude, the educator may choose not to spend her time with or for your child.

Attitude is a function of discontent. What is the catalyst for this attitude? How can you resume being the greatest influence over your child's life? This may become personal. Remember your child is depending on you for guidance. Let us try the following to resume our role as parent-advocate-leader-influencer for which you are responsible. Is your child's attitude your fault? Not necessarily. You may not be to blame, but you are responsible for the results of his/her attitude. In order to change the attitude, we must consider the following:

1. What is on her mind?

2. What does your child like?

3. Does he write to express himself? Do you read what she writes?

4. How much time do you spend texting your child? Do you know what all of the acronyms mean?

5. How much time do you spend talking to your child?

6. Does your child hear 'I love you' regularly enough?

## A Family's Guide for Success

7. What other compliments do you give your child? On a regular basis?

8. What happened for you to take a backseat in your child's life?

9. When was the last time you and your child spent quality time together – as defined by the child?

10. Who are her friends?

11. Who are his friends' parents?

12. What did you do to show interest and investment in his life today?

13. What part of the family is she responsible for?

14. What do you talk to your child about?

15. What does she want to talk to you about but that topic renders you speechless and distant?

16. Are you the parent that you always wanted or are you the one they hate?

17. Does your child respect your judgment and information and intellect?

18. Are you the source of her information? When she is curious, does she start with you? Or are you trumped by the internet?

19. What does he feel is in front of (more important than) him?

## ARE YOU READY FOR 9ᵀᴴ GRADE ... AGAIN?

20. Does she feel worthy of your time?

21. Does she know that you believe in her?

22. Does she think that you are approachable and reachable?

23. What can you do to improve her perception?

So within that series of questions are a few issues that we will consider. Your investment needs to increase in your child. The bottom line is to help the child understand her worth and help her overcome the obstacles she faces. She needs to know that she can trust you for her needs and concerns. Yes, as the parent, you do provide. Yes, you do work daily. Yes, you do provide a roof and food and clothes and gadgets. Those details do not constitute parenting. That is a confusing point however that is not the definition of parenting.

Add some time during your day for your child. Concern yourself with what concerns your child. Consider what she needs before you make decisions. Keep her in mind when you make plans. Make a date with him. This is basic—what you have always done. This needs to be different—intentional, purposeful. You are in competition for your child's heart, mind and soul. Some parents are not aware of that fact. Our influence over our children needs to be understood as paramount. They need us to PARENT.

## A FAMILY'S GUIDE FOR SUCCESS

Remember that they learned everything by mimicking us. What are we sharing now through our own attitude about school, achievement and life in general? Consider your parents. Are they achievers? Do they exhibit excellence? Do they share valuable information? Do you use the advice of others' parents more than your own? Does your child feel the same way about you? We need to be the AUTHORITY in their lives. This does not mean that we need to know everything. It does mean that our children check all of their information through us. We need to be their source. We are the gatekeeper of their hearts, minds, and important matters.

Improving your attitude and hers will increase the possibility of achievement and accomplishment. Likewise, when your attitude improves, you can hold them more highly accountable than before.

Some students use your attitude and behavior as an excuse not to achieve and to behave poorly. So consider carefully answering those questions so that you can start to change and challenge your child toward excellence. Please do not let your attitude wreck your education or that of your child's.

## What They Are Not Saying!

**(So what is your child saying by what they are not saying?)**

Your child, your student, needs to be successful. They are not telling us everything. They are not saying that they are discouraged. They are not

## ARE YOU READY FOR 9ᵀᴴ GRADE... AGAIN?

saying that they are hurt. They are not saying that they do not believe in themselves. They are omitting that they are struggling with particular concepts. They are not sharing that they have low self-esteem. They are not sharing that they are being pressured to not perform well academically. They are not sharing that they are being bullied nor that they are being pressured to have sex. They are not saying that they are missing the concepts. They are not telling that they feel all alone.

They are not talking because they do not feel like anyone is listening. They do not feel like they are important. They do not think that they are loved. They are not confident in what they feel and think is important.

Keep in mind that your child omits facts and details from their day. How do you get that crucial information from them in order to know how to help them with such difficulties? The first answer is that we remember what we needed as a teen. Realizing that this may be a painful experience. However, your child needs to be rescued in a manner you only wished for as a child. As a caring, responsible parent, we should seek to provide a solution to their insecurities, concerns, needs and differences. Your child needs help with life – school and academics are just details. They are not talking, so we need to help them speak. We need to help them know how to start difficult, confrontational conversations with you and other adults.

Some conversation starters:

# A Family's Guide for Success

- What did you learn today (specific subject)?

- How is (teacher name)?

- What did you eat for lunch?

- What is the best part of your day? Why?

- Consider what you need to be successful. Tell me.

- Who of your friends skip classes?

- What do you want to do with your life? Career?

- What was your favorite subject today?

- What were you successful with today?

- Who of your classmates is dating?

- Who of your classmates have parents who are divorced?

- Who of your classmates have tried drugs?

- Who of your classmates have tried or are having sex?

- Who of your friends have grandmothers?

- Who are your friends? Names? Where do you live?

## ARE YOU READY FOR 9<sup>TH</sup> GRADE ... AGAIN?

- What topic(s) do you need to discuss that you think is hard to talk about with me?

- What are your goals? Dreams?

- What do you want to accomplish with your life?

- What about your life is difficult?

- What about your life do you really like?

- Do you think that I'm a good parent? Why or why not?

- Could you be a better child/student? How?

- What does it take to be successful in this world?

- Why are you emotional about your education?

    This is not a comprehensive list; however, it will start the much-needed dialogue. This should start to solve some things that have been previously an issue. This will offer your student a platform for much-needed communication. With the improvement of your communication, the achievement expectation could be addressed and engaged. This will also help you say the things that you as the parent need to start saying because you too have left some things unsaid.

A FAMILY'S GUIDE FOR SUCCESS

**Affirmation**

The definition of affirmation is the act of affirming. To affirm is to validate or state positively. Affirmations are designed to encourage, uplift and confirm. Your child needs affirmation! She needs words that will lift her spirits and offer encouragement. He needs to know that he can overcome his issues. He needs words to build his confidence for the difficult situations he faces. She needs some words – from you – that will equip her for the tough times ahead. These words of affirmation will enhance his self-esteem to an operable state so that daily life is not a strain.

These affirmations influence success. These affirmations share with your child who she is. He will remember those positive words which serve to override those negative ones. You do not know when the negative will happen nor from where it will come. He needs a positive word bank so when he is discouraged he has something positive to access. He can counteract that negativity and will not lose heart. His access to some positive words may make the difference between his success versus him quitting, and whether temporarily or permanently. Your voice can be heard in his mind.

**ARE YOU READY FOR 9TH GRADE... AGAIN?**

"THE PURPOSE OF EDUCATION IS TO REPLACE AN EMPTY MIND WITH AN OPEN ONE."

MALCOLM S. FORBES

**A FAMILY'S GUIDE FOR SUCCESS**

Are You Ready for 9th Grade... Again?

# Achievement: A Matter of Legacy

**Matter of Legacy**

Achievement can be theoretically traced back to a hereditary source. The achievement and the academic success we desire for our students is a family matter. The matter of achievement comes from the parents and grandparents of the students. When you have achievers in the family, the expectation is that the student will also achieve. No matter what has previously happened, achievement can still happen as a matter of legacy.

Our students achieve because we make it important and we facilitate that process. This also means that you give your student permission to achieve. You may be thinking what does that mean. Students do not have any incentive to achieve more than you did unless you give them that consent as well as the necessary encouragement to do so.

In the Hispanic culture, the norm is that no child achieves more than the oldest patriarch or matriarch. A student shared this detail, and her parent confirmed the statement. The parent did not realize that her daughter felt that way. You can imagine the difference when the parent told the daughter that she was expected to attend and graduate from college. The daughter changed her entire educational approach. The mom considered returning to college. These

## A Family's Guide for Success

two steps fueled her toward success. Authorize your child to achieve. That authorization has so much power coming from you.

You have intense, personal influence over this road to achievement: use it well, wisely and often. What does this mean? You plan what your student will achieve, and you set forth a plan for doing so.

### What Will He Hear?

If you do not know how to affirm your child, there are resources that will assist you in what you need. The most important words that you can ever say are: I love you, I believe in you, I believe you, I want the best for you, I fully support you, and I think you are capable of success and achievement. When you tell your child those words, in an authentic voice with a genuine heart, then you are affirming your child. When your child is secure in your love, you will get all of who they are.

The other method for affirming your child is your complete transparency. When you reveal who you are – your struggles, your achievements, your pain, and your regrets – your child will then know that it is okay to achieve, to struggle, to strive, to create and to believe. You are the key to your child's belief system. You can drive your student's story by sharing your own. You can challenge the heart of your child by sharing your authentic self. Tell your child the stories you have never told anyone. Tell your child your fears that you have never shared with anyone. Bond in a way that will overwhelm even you. Put all that you are on the line for your child's experience.

Your affirmation of your child will show her your belief in an extravagant manner. She deserves you to bear your soul and mind and memories in a pure way that only your child can appreciate and deserves. Your affirmations override the foolishness to which they are exposed.

**Encouragement**

If you have not encouraged your child, then start with an apology for not doing so. Likewise, realize that your child depends on your voice. Your child needs your encouragement. Your voice needs to be the loudest, most predominant voice in her head.

Your encouragement should outweigh that of any other voice she hears. Remember when you wanted to hear your parent's voice or feel their support of being confident that they would appear in support of you? Maybe that is not our story but for many parents, this is your exact story and maybe worse. Change your child's legacy and experience. ENCOURAGE her by just showing up. Let your encouragement weigh more that his situation and circumstances.

Encouragement also translates into advocating for your child's success. In education, it is learning how to get past 'no,' and the other emotional and

## A Family's Guide for Success

mental obstacles that normally go unspoken. The student is a fragile element. She is emotional. He is experiencing poverty. The student needs some processing time to understand the new role, the new position and the exponentially higher expectations and qualifications.

You are developing a child into an adult human being, who will grow up to be the parent and will repeat this process. You are in charge of which process she repeats.

Do you remember your friends or maybe yourself saying that when I grow up and as a parent I will not do _____? Remember our children are making those same declarations. Remember how many of those promises you kept. As we grow older and more mature, we reconsider those statements. Help your child to understand why you do what you do – what is best, including understanding how your parents raised you.

Some of our educational woes are the result of someone keeping their promises. That promise does not necessarily mean it is a good thing. The person who reduced the importance of homework was sadly mistaken. We do not want to keep repeating these same errors.

### A Matter of Purpose

What is the purpose of this achievement? The purpose for achievement is she needs this achievement for her future. He does not know that he will need

## ARE YOU READY FOR 9ᵀᴴ GRADE . . . AGAIN?

any of this material later and at some critical moments. One critical place is as a parent. Did you think about needing to learn math better because you may have to help your own child with her homework? You may not have thought about it at age 14, however, not knowing is detrimental to the self-esteem of the student and the parent. There is an old adage that states: "It is better to have it and not need it than to need it and not have it." This supports the new adage that states: "Instruction doesn't come to an unprepared mind." Our children need education for many reasons: work, working in a competitive environment, successful school career and as a parent.

This achievement is purposed and planned. As you groom that achievement, you groom her life. You are creating an achiever who will birth and create more achievers. You have launched a change agent in our society. You have challenged societal norms with an educated answer for the lack of educated young people.

It is heart breaking to see a child who was never prepared for their life, and they desire a life that the world has decided that they are ill-equipped to have. This is based on knowledge and education and intelligence. This is arrived at through the grade point system. There are many children who grow up unprepared for the work force and do not possess enough skills to be successful in an office environment.

## A Family's Guide for Success

Our children need a blueprint for success. We need to ensure we instill in them the importance of several places for career options. There will always be engineering and accounting positions. There are certain careers that are plentiful, and some are not. Keep in mind that you and your child's options need to be open. Keep several options. Math and English are important in any position. Communication is important in every career. Those are basics. Energy needs to be spent in the future of the job market needs. There are studies and research that shares information where occupational needs will exist by the time your child graduates. This information will provide useful information so that you may help select the best major in college with the best minor for the plan B.

Purpose is intentional. Purpose is intentional planning, making use of all available tools that you can help your child find her gifts and his talents. There are tests and surveys which test their areas of interests and which match those interests with careers. Using this tool may be an indication of how to be satisfied with the use of your talents. Purpose makes the best career choice.

Purposeful achievement drives a successful child and a well-prepared adult.

The Most Influential Person In Your Child's Life

# ARE YOU READY FOR 9TH GRADE... AGAIN?

You as the parent of the child are the most influential person in her life. You have the power of persuasion, and you established expectations in his life. A word of caution: the only way to have this is to be present, doing your job actively. When you start asking questions or making suggestions but you start to hear other people's names, like a teacher or a counselor, that person has more influence than you. Tread cautiously here. The only way for another person to gain that position is because you were away from your post. Keep focused on being the parent. The one your child needs.

## Make A Poster: Past, Present and Future

The poster is a goal/dream poster. This poster outlines the PLAN for your student. The student needs to see the plan daily, and you need to see it as well as so everyone stays focused on the plan.

The poster outlines the goals:

- The degree we will graduate with

- The GPA we need to be admitted to the college of our choice

- The college list with photos of the college

- The SAT/ACT score needed

## A Family's Guide for Success

- The dates the test is/are offered: circling the date we will take the exam (we will take it a few times before we need the score); practice does the mind good

- Picture of parents and family who have graduated

- Picture of child in graduation robe – borrow one; find a frame or create an image with the class year on the photo

- The amount of money we need to attend those colleges

- The plan for how we are going to pay for that education

    o   Financial aid

    o   Savings

    o   Sports, music, academic, scholarship

- Dates to visit those campuses – needs to be part of family vacation plan

- Pictures of key personnel on campus (VP of Student Affairs, VP of Academic Affairs, President, Director of Admissions, any other staff you will meet or need to meet.)

- Pictures/list of what any rewards are (electronic gadgets, car, clothes, etc.) – these rewards are because you will meet the milestones

- List of your proudest moments – ask other family to add

## ARE YOU READY FOR 9ᵀᴴ GRADE... AGAIN?

The poster is designed to encourage, remind, redirect and reward for the past, present and future activities, achievements, and accomplishments. The poster needs a space to record the greatest results, post the report cards, teacher comments, and other progress.

Take a photo of the poster and give a copy to each teacher for all four years. This shares with the teacher what the goals are so that the teacher can be a stakeholder. As a stakeholder by definition means that you are invested as the teacher. You are gathering investors for your child. This poster is designed to instill hope for your child – regardless of the previous performance.

This poster gives your child the VIEW that achievement is more than possible; achievement is imminent! Belief starts when you have a clear view of where you are headed. When you get used to receiving praise, the more you want to hear and earn that praise. The poster has to be true! Make it true! Pursue the content of that poster!

**A FAMILY'S GUIDE FOR SUCCESS**

## Are You Ready for 9ᵗʰ Grade... Again?

"CHILDREN DEPRIVED OF WORDS BECOME SCHOOL DROPOUTS; DROPOUTS DEPRIVED OF HOPE BEHAVE DELINQUENTLY. AMATEUR CENSORS BLAME DELINQUENCY ON READING IMMORAL BOOKS AND MAGAZINES, WHEN IN FACT, THE INABILITY TO READ ANYTHING IS THE BASIC TROUBLE."

PETER S. JENNISON

## A Family's Guide for Success

ARE YOU READY FOR 9ᵀᴴ GRADE ... AGAIN?

# Conflict Management

**Conflict Resolution**

Children have tempers and express anger and express jealousy and show anxiety and fear all differently. Children are cruel to each other, often without cause. Because of clothes, hair, skin tone, ethnicity, speech, intelligence, special needs, physical attributes, and whatever other reason they can think of to tease each other. This is also labeled as bullying.

Children do not have great conflict resolution coping mechanisms. They do not naturally resort to conflict management or negotiations. They, usually, immediately fight. This fighting could include actual fighting or some other retaliatory behavior.

We have to teach conflict resolution. We teach adults, so we know children are not born with this skill. How do you groom your child not to fight, not to retaliate when he is hit, and not to provoke a fight? That is a difficult dynamic to address in a singular situation. You need to know some details about your child before any advice is given.

1. Does your child anger easily?

2. Is your child moody, or suffers from mood swings?

# A Family's Guide for Success

3. Does your child "play well with others?"

4. Does your child have a temper?

5. Does your child respond well to criticism?

6. Is your child argumentative?

7. Is your child mild mannered?

8. What was the nature of your child's last tantrum?

The questions are not comprehensive, but they give some insight into how conflict will be handled while not necessarily being resolved.

Teaching your child how to manage conflict is useful immediately. This needs to include coaching and role playing. It is so important that it is pivotal in success—now and in the future. Likewise, the coaching needs to include being present when your child needs to resolve conflict with adults, where you serve as a witness to the encounter rather than the resolution. This is a necessary activity. The child needs to feel empowered and equipped to address others in a respectful, progressive manner when all parties feel that their needs have been addressed.

If you do not feel equipped to handle this education, please seek a professional organization to help develop your child. Being able to resolve

## Are You Ready for 9th Grade... Again?

conflict well is/are the best skills they will ever have. It also will improve your relationship with your child.

**Fights Cost Money**

In the "old" days, specifically 1989 and before, a fight at school resulted in suspension at home and lost of grades for the days of school missed, without the opportunity to make up any of it.

At some point, this changed. The policy was extended to being issued a ticket which included a monetary fine, a court appearance and additional school days missed to appear in court. The parent has to appear as well. An attorney may need to be retained. You can see that this has an expense attached. This process could have attached probation time and a label on your criminal history.

Do you understand how important great conflict resolution is? Our successful, achieving student cannot be persuaded to throw all or a percentage of that away because of some foolishness that should be solved with words.

Many parents are surprised at all of the infractions that can earn your child, and consequently your family, a citation. Foul language is one such offense. If your student curses in the presence of, at the teacher, or directly to a teacher, staff member or/and administrator, she can get a ticket by the campus police officer. That citation starts the process outlined for the fight.

## A FAMILY'S GUIDE FOR SUCCESS

The details can be found in the education code for your state, under the code of disorderly conduct. Keep in mind that our goal is education. We cannot get side tracked with the "disruptive" label.

Know that the ticket costs money. Do you really want to pay for that? Do you understand that those costs takeaway from the family budget, which may already be stretched? Your family cannot afford to spend any money on this venture. This money spent because of your poor behavior could be used to pay the light bill or the car insurance. So in short, BEHAVE! Stop misbehaving in school and at home. It is expensive, and it is untimely and ineffective.

Most poor behavior is a result of wanting attention. If you want the attention of your parents or you teacher, then ASK! Stop acting out! Stop fighting! Stop causing trouble!

Just a note parents: when children fight in school and it is recorded on their cell phones, it can and will be used in a court of law. When children fight within 500 yards of the school, the authority rests with the schools and is still punishable by the district police and school administration.

Further, fighting is distracting from an educational perspective because you will be suspended from school for at least one day. This absence means that your student will miss important instruction that impacts the total educational experience.

## ARE YOU READY FOR 9ᵀᴴ GRADE... AGAIN?

**Language Costs Money**

If your child chooses to curse an adult on a campus, your child can be ticketed which has a fine associated with it.

Please remind your child that foul language is inappropriate and costly. It also erases the teacher/student relationship. Often this relationship is not properly renewed. The use of profanity means that we lack the vocabulary you need to communicate your disappointment and frustration.

**Student/Teacher Communication**

The teacher communication with your student is a daily situation. They need a great relationship. The parent needs to facilitate that relationship. How do we do that?

Parents, we are to have a great relationship first. That means that parents are communicating regularly with both the student and the teacher. Whether the communication is via email or phone or in person, the parent needs to facilitate that relationship. This includes sharing with each party how to manage successfully the other person and their personalities. Specifically that means the parent shares with the teacher how to satisfy the needs of your child and how to successfully educate your child. This information needs to be shared in a transparent manner so that the student is affirmed through that information. Likewise, the student is being coached to speak well to the teacher.

# A Family's Guide for Success

One parent taught the author that the parent's positioning is key for the success of the student. This parent was phenomenal. She labeled her parent/teacher conference as a "begging session." She positioned herself in this meeting as the mediator/advocate. She was honest about her objectives.

She apologizes for her son's behavior. She takes notes on what he needs to do to catch up in class. She moved the meeting at an awesome pace. The author left the meeting awarding her with the parent of the year. The teachers sat in awe of her in a respectable manner. The level of investment of both the teachers and the student increased higher than ever. The accountability increased as well. The teachers knew that they needed to do more and the student know he needed to do so as well. The parent met several objectives in a VERY surprising manner.

The parent needs this relationship to thrive without her constant supervision. The parent cannot monitor the total relationship daily.

The student needs to be coached on how to interact with the teacher. The student needs to be able to ask:

1. What is my current grade?

2. What do I need to do to improve my grade?

3. What do you recommend I do to be successful?

## Are You Ready for 9th Grade... Again?

4. What do I do well?

5. What do I need to improve?

6. Can you help me become a better student?

7. Can you help me become the student you can mentor and write a recommendation letter for?

8. Are you respectful in your speech and your approach?

9. Do you understand that the teacher has resources that you need?

10. Do you understand that whether you like the teacher or not has nothing to do with how the teacher can help you?

11. Do you understand the value of your education and the value of the teachers among us?

The teacher does need to impact a life – your student's! The teacher needs to inspire your student. The teacher needs to be inspired to serve your student. The teacher creates some energy within your student. The teacher needs to be motivated to do so. The teacher is paid to teach. The teacher needs to be inspired to help and invest in your student. You need to remember to make that easy for the teacher. A teacher is a person and has to be respected and regarded as a person with feelings and shortcomings.

## A Family's Guide for Success

Parents, you are solely responsible for the successful communication between the two of them. Keep this communication going.

By the way, you as the parent have to ensure that you require balance. One parent told the author that the teacher and the child were having a personality conflict. This comment was inappropriate. The parent has allowed the child to think that he was equal to that teacher. The error in this philosophy is that the teacher is being disrespected, and the parent is consenting to the disrespect and participating in that disrespect. This path of disrespect distracted him from his much-needed education. He was a failing student and she used valuable time during a parent-teacher-student conference to discuss his twelve-year-old personality conflict, rather than how she could help improve his academic standing. When she shared that the child "did not hate" the teacher, the teacher stated that your feelings are irrelevant. The teacher further explained that education comes before emotion even in the dictionary. The teacher insisted that the student and the parent should place their feelings to the side so that the student could learn.

Your child's education cannot be interrupted with some misplaced emotions. This kind of interruption will cause your students' education to derail, and you create a false reality. You have not shown your student how to appropriately manage his emotions. This is not an issue of conflict or conflict resolution. It is a horrible placement of emotion.

## ARE YOU READY FOR 9ᵀᴴ GRADE ... AGAIN?

Parent, you have to remain focused and keep your child focused. You are HERE to LEARN! Nothing less!

You are responsible for this communication. You are also accountable for the student's communication. This communication is coaching for the now and the future.

**A FAMILY'S GUIDE FOR SUCCESS**

## ARE YOU READY FOR 9TH GRADE... AGAIN?

"EDUCATION IS A PROGRESSIVE DISCOVERY OF OUR OWN IGNORANCE."

WILL DURANT

## A Family's Guide for Success

Are You Ready for 9th Grade... Again?

# The Successful 9th Grader

**How to Measure**

The successful 9th grader is measured by grades and behavior. The grades reflect effort and diligence. While the grades may not be all A's or honor roll, we measure progress. Is your student improving on every grading period? If not, why not? What can we do to help your student to improve? Effort is measured by your improvement. This is done by increasing the grade during every grading period. When you remain the same from grade period to another also exerts effort. In math, in particular, because the material changes between grading cycles the material will present a challenge. The goal is not to drop below the previous cycle.

This also means that the student needs to ask periodically (every two weeks) what her grade is. Diligence is how hard your student is moving toward the goal to good grades and excellent test scores.

Further, the 9th grader needs to seek help and communicate. Communication is key to the teacher and parent. A successful 9th grader shares the issues he is having in class authentically. The student needs to be honest with the teacher when he is having trouble with the concepts presented and share

# A FAMILY'S GUIDE FOR SUCCESS

with the parent the same conversation, as well as asking for and anticipating the parents' support.

The student should ask for help immediately. Do NOT wait until test week to share that you do not understand anything that has been taught over the last six weeks. The student should ask for help, find a tutor or study group for the educational gaps.

Once we consider the educational gaps for the student, we have to assess that student for her strengths. Likewise, we need to consider the weaknesses. As the parent and advocate, we need to be prepared in those difficult subject areas so that we are also being proactive.

As you are checking the class work and reviewing the test scores, ask questions like:

1. How comfortable do you feel about (each subject)? On a scale from 1 to 10.

2. When do you need my help/interaction?

3. Have you spoken to your teacher? What did she say?

4. Teach the topic in a way you understand it from your classroom.

5. Would a parent-teacher-student conference be necessary?

6. Are you giving it all that you have?

## Are You Ready for 9th Grade... Again?

7. Are you discouraged? When did that take place?

8. Do you know that I care?

As for the successful, behaved 9th grader, that student is respectful, kind, attentive to directions, and is a good listener. The behaved student pays attention in class, focuses on the lesson and retains the information presented.

The behaved child is an art because we are not referring to perfect; there are not perfect children. We are growing and grooming good citizens. We want to share socially acceptable behavior that we can be proud of now and later. If we train our children, then we will be confident about how they will perform as an adult.

When we consider the details and characteristics of a responsible adult who is working, educated at some level, and parent's responsibly, we are the outcome of someone's effort. As an adult, we are someone's report card as well. What is our grade?

## What Does That Look Like

A respectful child speaks to adults respectfully and politely. She will use polite words and a polite tone and a good attitude. Most of the complaints about teenagers are that they are rude and disrespectful. The adults want to be regarded highly. In order for those to happen simultaneously, the effort has to

## A Family's Guide for Success

be mutual. The teenagers we know and love need an understanding of why respect is required and earned. It is hard to measure a students' respect.

Tone is defined the way something is said. Most of our students need to realize that what comes out of their mouth matches what is on their minds. There may be no diplomacy attached to it. We are coaching the students so when the "tone" has the potential to offend you, stop and coach them to success. When we are teaching and coaching young people, we need to incorporate the "whys." Share with her why that tone is disrespectful. Encourage her to calm down before she speaks. This is critical when we are coaching the teenager. We also need to praise her when she gets it right. Tone is subjective. We want to coach compassionately and consistently.

Body language is just as subjective, and coaching becomes important here as well. Great body language coaching shares negative and positive observations evenly. Again, the "why's" are important. Further with body language, share observations and what conclusions can be drawn from the body language. Use others as well as hers to share those observations. Giving her this knowledge will help her make the best choices and decisions.

Attitude has to be the most subjective of it all. The actual observations related to attitude are perceived. Attitude is defined as manners, disposition, feeling, posture in response to a person or thing, and response to emotion. So with that said, attitude is judged by what is thought about another's emotions.

## Are You Ready for 9th Grade... Again?

Again, coaching is important here. There are "whys" that is needed to help our students understand that an attitude needs to be managed carefully. Again, coaching is important.

**Do As I Do**

Parents, also during this season, it is critical you understand your impact on the behavior of our students. Many times students are expecting you to arrive on campus argumentative and confrontational. We need to understand that you influence the behavior of your child based on our own behavior. The student expects you to behave regularly, which in this case is poorly. You have to own the part of their behavior which they "inherited." They mimic what they know and what they see. If you behave in a questionable, argumentative or confrontational manner, you can expect your child to do the same.

If this is your story, start with yourself. Please understand that if your behavior is this way, your child does not think anything is wrong with his behavior because the two of you behave the same. When a child uses language like "my mother is going to handle you," or "my mother does not care about that," the parent needs to address the behavior. The school should not have to bear the student's burdens, and certainly, not alone. If your child's behavior continues, the staff and administrator should divest in your child. Your conversation is not "that's not fair – they better _____," rather it is your responsibility to insure that your child overcomes that behavior. The

## A Family's Guide for Success

administration develops this image of you through your behavior; that image does not help your child.

**Attendance, Dress Code, and Work Ethic**

Attendance is required for graduation and class credit. Many students lose credits because they "miss" classes – unexcused absences. These absences impact your child's education, the retention of material, the practice of material and the successful completion of all required course work. Please understand that you are a parent and are responsible, so check on your child's attendance regularly so that you are not surprised if this starts to happen. Share with your student what attendance means to their success. Remember, these are life-long lessons, not temporary ones. By the way, poor attendance could land you in court with additional expenses.

Dress code is required. Keeping a neat appearance is attached to self-respect and self-esteem. We are building our future. We are supposed to hold them accountable for this activity. The dress code has to be adhered to. If not, similar disciplinary action can take place.

In one school, there was a young lady who wore a very short dress. When she was asked about it, she said her mother did not care what she wore. When she was sent to the principal's office, she then offered to change clothes. She had other clothes in her backpack that means that she knew her clothes were

## ARE YOU READY FOR 9ᵀᴴ GRADE... AGAIN?

too short, and she was willing to challenge authority. The teacher called the mother. During the conversation, the teacher realized that the parent did indeed care and was unaware that her child was changing clothes at school. Further, the mother was surprised that her daughter thought this incident would go unnoticed by her and the adults around her.

The teacher continued to invest in her because of the mother's investment, which was quite different from what the child shared. Dress code is an expression for an internal feeling. The dress code rebellion completely communicates that the child craves attention only brought on by breaking the dress code or other rules. What other attention can fulfill that need? Only you can determine that through observation and communication.

Work ethic is practical and developed through all influential parties based on established standards. Our students develop work ethic by sharing the standards of excellence. Work ethic defined by Gage as working diligently, arriving to class on time, completing all assignments, seeking help if necessary, checking on their own progress and working hard without excuse. You teach and hold them accountable the exact same way! Show, practice, repeat. Show them each step and each detail. You watch while they practice. Give them your feedback. Encourage her success. Repeat the lesson if it was not successful. Start with a new topic if the last one was successful.

## A FAMILY'S GUIDE FOR SUCCESS

This work ethic is again for the future as well; learned, practiced and mastered under your watchful eye. Sometimes, young people do not think that you have any work ethic. They consider the teacher's expectations new and unreasonable. Change those expectations to yours. Help your student to understand that you expect a respectable work ethic. Again, work ethic is a life-long need and most effective when you initiate the lessons and set the expectations. The rest of us are just accessories.

**80%, 85%, 90%, 95%, and 100%**

The successful 9th grader is successful based on:

- Completing 90% of the homework

- Completing 100% of the classwork

- Completing 100% exams

- Attending 100% tutorials when help is needed

- Practicing to stay sharp when help is not necessary

- Maintain a 90% average in all classes

- Earning 100% in all electives, especially physical education

- Use 100% of your mind

## ARE YOU READY FOR 9ᵀᴴ GRADE ... AGAIN?

- Give 100% effort on every occasion

- Quit 0% of the time

- Ask enough questions to get a complete understanding

- Is polite

- Manages tone, body language and attitude

- Desires knowledge

- Wants to learn

- Wants to be successful

- Has 95% attendance

- Has 100% dress code

- Realizes that 100% of this is for them, the student

- Realizes that success is determined by the educator, parent and student but judged by the world

- Seeking excellence

- Concerned with overall school experience

- Completing all necessary credits for 9th grade on time

## A FAMILY'S GUIDE FOR SUCCESS

- Have a great opinion of yourself

- Others encourage you

- Others have a great opinion of you

- Keep a positive attitude about all situations

- Do your best daily!

- Be an example for other students

- Encourages others

- Keep that going for the next three years!

### Are You Ready for 9th Grade... Again?

"EDUCATION BREEDS CONFIDENCE. CONFIDENCE BREEDS HOPE. HOPE BREEDS PEACE."

CONFUCIUS

**A FAMILY'S GUIDE FOR SUCCESS**

## ARE YOU READY FOR 9ᵀᴴ GRADE... AGAIN?

# 10th, 11th, and Senior Year:

## What Happens If We Need to Catch Up

The standard graduation age is 18 years old. This is based on starting school at six years old in kindergarten, not repeating any grades. There are times when a student may get behind for some reason.

We want the student to complete school. We need to catch-up so that we do not get discouraged. We also do not want to always offer the GED option. So we need to catch-up by the use of the internet through virtual school, summer school, high school, and community college. Further, the school district may also offer some credit makeup classes.

Even if we are not making up but rather getting even and improving your GPA, there are vehicles to do this: summer school, virtual school and community college.

If summer school is available, go every summer and complete a subject. The author recommends history or science, based on your student's favorite subjects. When you are taking these classes, the author recommends that your student take the same topic throughout. For instance, history and all social studies are good for consistency. Please consider carefully not switching to English and Math. This is going to interrupt the educational flow. Math has

## A FAMILY'S GUIDE FOR SUCCESS

building principles which will be missed in summer school if you choose to take one math class in the regular year and then go to summer school for a second class and then return to the regular classroom. There may be some details that cannot be covered in a summer school class. But whatever you do, try to do all of the credits of that topic.

Online as well is a great use of time. Both of these options would be beneficial for the student trying to improve the GPA and overcome the subject matter anxiety as well.

Any core college courses can be transferred to almost anywhere from the local junior college. This reduces the time and money spent in college; sometimes you can achieve dual credit for both college and high school. Research is definitely required. This path-way gives your student what he needs to move into the leader role in his own life.

What you do today will make your life easier later. If you pay into that credit bank consistently, then you will graduate early or maybe on time. You can then monitor the college credits. If you can transfer 15-18 hours, which is 5-6 classes, then you have one semester done.

Keep in mind that same summer school advice applies. Likewise, the online portion is definitely a bonus! Between the work ethic and the diligence, your student will understand how to overcome any obstacles and certainly use

## ARE YOU READY FOR 9ᵀᴴ GRADE... AGAIN?

the available options to benefit him. Her future is bright, and she might as well know it.

There is no shame in making up the time necessary. Encourage the student to move forward.

**A FAMILY'S GUIDE FOR SUCCESS**

## Are You Ready for 9ᵗʰ Grade... Again?

"EDUCATION IS THE POWER TO THINK CLEARLY, THE POWER TO ACT WELL IN THE WORLD'S WORK, AND THE POWER TO APPRECIATE LIFE."

BRIGHAM YOUNG

# A Family's Guide for Success

ARE YOU READY FOR 9ᵀᴴ GRADE . . . AGAIN?

# It's Not That Long – 4 More Years

These are the fastest four years ever! The author admits that four years will be full but fast. This is the most important four years of her childhood. This is the last chance to affect life decisions, establish work ethic, and start the student on the successful path.

This is like the anchor leg of any race. This is when you try everything, use all of your speed, and give it all of your energy and effort. You do not win the relay by conserving energy. These four years are critical, and they require your attention. This is a planned time in your lives when some things cannot happen – there are no more unplanned school absences. This is going to be strictly planned time, where we do not have any unnecessary traveling and extracurricular activities. The decision is made by asking yourself does this activity propel my student forward or is this essential to the education or is this a once in a lifetime experience or does this experience interfere with something important we need to complete.

This is a critical time. You do not get any do-overs so treat this race with immense care.

**What Happens During This Time?**

## A Family's Guide for Success

Create a list of colleges you and your child might like to attend. Ten schools. A pure dream list. No school is impossible! Write them down. My list reads Stanford, American University, University of California at Berkeley, Princeton, Northwestern University, Rice, Pepperdine, Harvard, Georgetown, and University of Miami.

When we view this list, we are making a list with the following information: application due date, application address – if web only, application fee, GPA average, SAT score, ACT score, length of essay, number of recommendations needed, contact information and any notes. This chart gives us a comparative tool of the schools as well as keeps up with dates in front of you. As we prepare for college, we prepare for the most difficult school. We reach for the highest numbers.

We also plan the extracurricular activities by year that the student will be involved. This chart eliminates the guessing that is associated with "I wonder if I can get in." As we progress, we know the goal, so it is easier to meet a desired goal, and then we have a real chance to reach it.

**The 4 Year Plan**

This aggressive approach needs to take the following steps. First, meet with the student's counselor to share the goal and the dynamics of the plan, asking for guidance and support. This meeting is critical as one of the letters of

## Are You Ready for 9th Grade ... Again?

recommendations will come from a counselor. The counselor is designed to help guide the student toward success. They HELP people who have REAL plans. They HELP people who have engaged and PRESENT parents! This means YOU! They do not help every student for which they are responsible and assigned. They do the class schedules for everyone. They do not help everyone. There is internal bias that limits their ability to help people who are not helping themselves. They use the criteria mentioned earlier about attendance, grades and attitude when determining who they believe will attend and be successful in college.

Second, have a parent-teacher-student conference where you share this same information with the teachers asking them to keep your child accountable, to share any valuable information with you regarding her work ethic, how much work needs to be done to EARN the A, seeking guidance for the path to success, and other keys to the student you desire. They also write recommendation letters.

Third, you need to know the advisor for the activities your student is a part of so that they can be instrumental with helping your child to become a leader in that organization. The leadership role makes a difference on the college application, rather than just being a member.

Fourth and finally, you are showing your child how to build relationships, teaching her how to ask for what she needs, and grooming him for

## A FAMILY'S GUIDE FOR SUCCESS

the excellence he needs. The administrative team needs to be included in the plan. The fact you are in a relationship with the administration speaks volumes to both parties. The student will be less likely to get in trouble. The administration will then understand that you care, and extra care will be taken if your child should have an infraction. Further, your student will know the level of accountability expected by all parties involved. There is power for you when at least ten people can say, "Stop misbehaving! You know your mother will be disappointed if we have to call her."

When you meet with all of them, you have changed the stereotype for your child and yourself as a parent.

The four-year plan includes outlining the courses for each semester including summer classes, virtual classes, and dual credit courses. The goal would be for 12-24 hours of dual credit. This needs to be in a visible place. Likewise, when the grade is earned, post the grade and calculate the GPA. Again, we need to remain focused on the goal. The visual means that we have the evidence of our efforts on the wall.

There will be trends which show us which topics are best for the student, as well as the least successful topics. The purpose of identifying these trends is so that we can determine what should be taken in summer or virtual school. This is designed to keep the GPA high.

## Are You Ready for 9th Grade... Again?

This aligns with the extracurricular activities as well. Please choose carefully.

Now we need visit the colleges – starting with the one you want to attend the most. These visits need to be announced, and a reservation made. This is your method of introducing your student to the college. The first time they see your child's name is on the application. This visit will distinguish your student from others. We are not in competition for admittance but money for school. We desire to attend college for free.

Please establish a routine in your home. What time is bed time? Study time? Dinner time? Entertainment? Television on during the week versus weekend? Again, this requires your discipline too. It may mean that you are at the study table as well – whatever it takes to help the student succeed.

Gather a team of tutors you can call for "on-call" support for any last minute questions the night before a test. We are planning for a successful four years, and we need an entire arsenal. The tutor may be free or for a charge – either way, be prepared to share with the tutor team the plan for the next four years.

The next four years will be intense, important, insightful, and invigorating. This will be a reminder of your personal experience – some great and some horrible. Be careful that you protect the current experience from your

# A Family's Guide for Success

vicarious living. Share all the memories possible and remember that this is your student's experience. Take lots of pictures!

Plan vacations that will add to her educational experience. Research will be required to know what countries, states and cities they will be studying and the settings of the literature they will read. The travel will add to the retention of the information being studied. It is the purposed art of intersecting the classroom with the playground.

Save money for the future. The senior year expenses should total $3420-4000. There are senior dues/fees, which should include: prom tickets ($250), yearbook ($80-$100), senior photos ($200), attire ($600-$800), transportation to the prom ($200), senior trip ($1200), and class ring ($400-$600). There needs to be a yearbook each year, so an additional $240-$300. You can consider how to rearrange those expenses however you see fit but do not let them be unexpected – these are the KNOWN fees. There will be some surprise events with fees associated with them, however if so, they will be events such as spring break travel.

Look forward with excitement. You will be a different parent and person based on this experience. Spend time researching scholarships for your student. This needs to start from day one of high school. We have a lot of work to do. Starting early provides advantage.

## Are You Ready for 9th Grade ... Again?

Start taking the SAT twice a year until we make the right score. Invest in the prep course. It will save you thousands later! You can start taking the SAT in the 7th grade. Practice eliminates test anxiety.

The other detail that needs to be mentioned: this preparation will insure that college is successful. There are too many stories about students who went to college, but did not finish, and all of this would be regretted. This four-year stint is designed to insure that the next four are great as well.

**A FAMILY'S GUIDE FOR SUCCESS**

"THE PRINCIPLE GOAL OF EDUCATION IN THE SCHOOLS SHOULD BE CREATING MEN AND WOMEN WHO ARE CAPABLE OF DOING NEW THINGS, NOT SIMPLY REPEATING WHAT OTHER GENERATIONS HAVE DONE; MEN AND WOMEN WHO ARE CREATIVE, INVENTIVE AND DISCOVERERS, WHO CAN BE CRITICAL AND VERIFY, AND NOT ACCEPT, EVERYTHING THEY ARE OFFERED."

JEAN PIAGET

**A FAMILY'S GUIDE FOR SUCCESS**

# Conclusion and Final Thoughts

Parents, I know that these four years have you concerned, consumed, and maybe even overwhelmed. There is hope! At the end of this book, you have learned, reflected and planned. Now the work begins but you are set-up and equipped for success.

Remember, this is a working document. You have to refer to the websites often for any updates and legislative changes that may be relevant to your child. This may seem like a full-time job because it is. However, the outcome will overwhelmingly pay you in the long-run.

When the days and work get tough, remember we cannot quit! I would love to hear from you – your stories and testimonials. Use this as encouragement that you will survive and be part of a great experience!

Keep in mind that the pay-off starts when they leave for college, and you go on vacation right after they graduate from high school. You will have earned it. The additional reward is that they go to school and call, text, email or video message you and say the magic words: "I get it!" Those are the words we are working for! Keep at it until you hear those words. Until then fall in love with your child's heart and education again.

# A Family's Guide for Success

# Resources

## Articles

"Our High Schools are a Disaster"

http://www.slate.com/articles/life/education/2014/02/high_school_in_america_a_complete_disaster.2.html

"The School that is Changing American Education" time.com/10038/the-school-that-is-changing-**american**-**education**/

A FAMILY'S GUIDE FOR SUCCESS

# Books

Motivating Students Who Don't Care: Successful Techniques for Educators Allen N. Mendler

What Great Teachers Do Differently: 14 Things That Matter Most Todd Whitaker

What's Worth the Fighting for Out There Andy Hargreavees; Michael Fullan

Failure is Not an Option Alan M. Blankstein

If You Don't Feed the Teachers, They Eat the Students Neila A. Connors

College Board SAT Prep

College Board ACT Prep

How Children Succeed: Grit, Curiosity, and the Hidden Power of Character Paul Tough

Classroom Instruction That Works: Research-Based Strategies for Increasing Student Achievement, 2nd edition  Ceri B. Dean, Elizabeth Ross Hubbell, Howard Pitler and and BJ Stone

Closing the Attitude Gap: How to Fire Up Your Students to Strive for Success  Baruti Kafele

ARE YOU READY FOR 9ᵀᴴ GRADE... AGAIN?

## Websites

National Board of Education     www.ed.gov

1. Massachusetts     www.doe.mass.edu
2. New York     schools.**nyc**.gov
3. Texas     www.tea.state.**tx**.us
4. Florida     www.fldoe.org
5. California     www.cde.**ca**.gov
6. Iowa     educateiowa.gov
7. Georgia     www.gadoe.org
8. Illinois     www.isbe.net
9. Delaware     www.doe.k12.de.us
10. North Carolina     www.ncpublicschools.org

# A Family's Guide for Success

# Acknowledgements

God, thank You for Your plans for me. Thank You for *Are You Ready for 9th Grade . . . Again? A Family's Guide to Success* and choosing me to complete Your project. I just want to please You. Thank You for continuing to anoint me and to invest in me and my gifts, which keep surprising me. Thank You for loving and forgiving me.

Hillary and Nehemiah, thank you for supporting me and my endeavors. Thank you for loving me, especially when I do nothing without a pen and a clipboard, thank you for enduring my late nights, your ideas, the sounding board, the love and the support. Thank you for celebrating our legacy.

Dr. Kimberly McLeod for all that you do and add to my life. Thank you for keeping the achievement bar high!

To my prayer partners and to my accountability partners, thank you for the long talks and the powerful prayers and the encouragement. To my pastor and church family, thank you so much for your love and support.

**A FAMILY'S GUIDE FOR SUCCESS**

The Educator is serious about her students and those who do not
know that their lives are at stake here.
Take this book and use it to grow for the betterment of your family.

A life-long learner who wants to inspire all students to learn, create
a legacy of achievement, and influence those children to hate math
a little bit less. She chases hearts and minds for an educated world.
She has educated over 3,000 students and will not quit.

The educator is educated and wants to inspire others to do the same.
With two Master's degrees and a Ph. D., she supports
Your quest for the same.

Contact the educator/author at
onediagage@onediagagespeaks.com
www.onediagagespeaks.com
@onediangage
Youtube.com/onediagage ♦ Blogtalkradio.com/onediagage
Facebook.com/onediagage

# A Family's Guide for Success

## Are You Ready for 9ᵗʰ Grade . . . Again?

## Advocate ♦ Teacher ♦ Parent Coach

To invite Ms. Gage to teach, advocate, and coach, please contact us at

@onediangage (twitter) ♦ onediagage@onediagagespeaks.com ♦

www.onediagagespeaks.com

facebook.com/onediagage educator page

**A FAMILY'S GUIDE FOR SUCCESS**

## ARE YOU READY FOR 9TH GRADE... AGAIN?

## Publishing

Do you have a book you want to write, but do not know what to do?

Do you have a book you need to publish but do not know how to start?

Would publishing move your career forward?

Let us help

onediagage@purpleink.net ♦ www.purpleink.net

# 281.740.5143 ♦ 512.715.4243

www.ingramcontent.com/pod-product-compliance
Lightning Source LLC
Chambersburg PA
CBHW031626160426
43196CB00006B/296